The
Divorced
Parent's
Challenge

EIGHT LESSONS TO TEACH
CHILDREN LOVE AND FORGIVENESS

Cheryl Grabenstein

The Divorced Parent's Challenge
Eight Lessons To Teach Children Love And Forgiveness
By Cheryl Grabenstein

ISBN: 978-0-9792044-0-1
Editor & Indexing: Christine Frank, www.ChristineFrank.com
Cover and Interior design: Toolbox Creative, www.ToolboxCreative.com

CONTENTS

- When you punish each other, you hurt your child
- No one can ever take your place
- There can never be too much love
- Do not compete with your child's other parent
- Work to form a bond with all the children in your life
- Forgetfulness damages relationships
- Accept that other caring adults can add to your child's happiness

- Place responsibility where it belongs
- Your anger is about you, not your child or your ex
- If you ignore your relationships, they will fall apart
- Honor your commitments
- It will not matter to your child who you think is at fault for your divorce
- If you let your children blame you, they will

Eight Challenges

Too often, following a divorce, parents attempt to punish each other and in the process add to the anguish of their children. This page helps illustrate the extremes that can exist for some divorced parents in their relationship with an ex-spouse. *"Moving right"* is accomplished when we focus on the love we feel for our children instead of the negative feelings we harbor toward an ex spouse.

The connection is through the child and when kept in the forefront of our minds, it becomes more difficult to take action against someone who cares about our children. Our unresolved issues should never deny our children the love and attention of other responsible adults. When you tackle this challenge, you and your child will experience more happiness.

Obsession ···➤ Focus

Punishment ···➤ Forgiveness

Indiscretion ···➤ Patience

Dishonesty ···➤ Integrity

Resentment ···➤ Loyalty

Resistance ···➤ Flexibility

Revenge ··➤ Satisfaction

Disrespect ··➤ Mutual Regard

Where do you fall?

WHERE DO YOU FALL?

The emotions on this page represent what happens when we attempt to punish an ex-spouse. As we *"move right"* our focus begins to return to our child.

"I come first"	*"What about my child?"*
"I want you to suffer for what happened to me."	"Nothing has changed the love we have for our child, but I want my child with me instead of my ex."
"This divorce was not my fault, and I am going to make sure everyone knows it."	"I know there are some things I need to apologize for, but I would rather not talk about my mistakes."
"I want to have some fun. I don't want to wait another minute."	"Maybe it will be different this time; even if it isn't, it will probably be okay."
"I need to make sure my child never knows what I have done wrong."	"I know I am not perfect, but it is easier to talk about other people than to admit my mistakes."
"My child doesn't need anyone but me."	"It is not easy to cooperate with my ex, but my child's needs are different than mine."
"I need to find someone new in a hurry. I don't want to look like a loser because I couldn't stay married."	"I am afraid to be alone."
"You owe me. I want you to pay for what I have been through."	"I worry about how I will get by with less money."
"I enjoy watching my ex struggle. He [she] deserves it."	"I am uncomfortable around people who seem to be doing better than I am."

Moving Right
Positive emotions encourage more happiness for everyone.

Eight principles for parents	*"I know I can do a better job"*
FOCUS Keep your eye on the child	"My child is lucky to have others, in addition to me, who care about him[her]."
FORGIVENESS Blame resolves nothing	"Everyone makes mistakes. The important thing is to accept imperfection while also striving to be a better person."
PATIENCE Maintain boundaries	"I do not need to share the adult details of my life with my child."
INTEGRITY Secrets destroy families	"I can find a way to tell my child the truth that is respectful of others."
LOYALTY The connection with an ex is through the child	"No one loves my child less because of the divorce. My feelings about my ex have nothing to do with my child."
FLEXIBILITY The past does not dictate the future	"I need to remember that my child is affected by the changes in my life."
SATISFACTION Money is not a weapon	"It is nice to have money but people are more important than things."
MUTUAL REGARD Value those who value your child	"My child benefits from the love and guidance of others. This can never take anything away from me."

Make the Right Move

Notes

Jerks of Divorce

Experiencing a divorce causes your life, as well as the lives around you, to be jerked in some way. You may have been caught by surprise or experienced reverberations you never imagined possible. If you have a child, he or she has also experienced jerks. A child's world is turned upside down for a period of time when his or her parents divorce. When a child's parents are not coping effectively with their divorce, the jerks are compounded.

Jerks can be experienced on several different levels. They can be physical or emotional. The word is also used to describe a person who acts like a jerk by behaving in self-serving ways. The waves of any of these jerks echo within us and around us. Consider the physical jerk of an auto accident. The body doesn't stop just because the automobile did. The impact causes injuries to the body, both internal and external. The black and blue of a bruise is a manifestation of physical trauma. The body asks for rest by aching, throbbing, and burning. Healing is enhanced by treating the body with care and respect.

When a jerk is experienced emotionally, there are no such outward manifestations, at least not ones that are immediately visible to others. Those who experience emotional jerking are bruised psychologically. A divorce causes these types of jerks. If you are divorced, you know what this means. So does your child.

I wrote this book because of what I have experienced professionally and personally. I was a registered nurse for twenty-five years and worked in maternal and child health. I have a graduate degree in counseling and focused my studies on parenting after divorce. My first husband Brad and I separated from each other when our oldest daughter was four years old and our youngest was barely five months of age. So I have been challenged by many of the concepts I present in these pages for more than twenty years.

In this book, I apply eight principles I have developed that I believe challenge most parents after a divorce. I understand that every divorce is different and that what worked for me may have little implication for you. But as you learn about your response to these challenges, your increased awareness will help you learn to pause before you react and ask yourself about your desired outcome. If you are focusing too much on your ex-spouse at the expense of your child, this book will help you learn to *move right* toward more positive emotion. In a nutshell, this book will help you be become more happily divorced.

Each chapter represents a lesson on the opportunity we have to *move right* from a negative, self-destructive response to a more positive one. My goal is to help the millions of divorced parents understand that whenever we react with vengeance toward someone who loves one of our children, we hurt our children as well as ourselves.

The goal to *"move right"* is summarized in chart form at the beginning of this book and then explored in each chapter. We *move to the right* by focusing on our child's

experience first and our own second. Do not take this to mean
I advocate making a child the center of your universe. I think
that is one of the most destructive things a parent can do.

Challenge One: Obsession versus Focus

Many parents lose focus, at least initially, when they
experience a divorce. To a degree, this is understandable.
Divorce is difficult for everyone, but it is made more difficult
for a child when parents become lost in their own world.
These are the parents who are acting like jerks toward their
child's other parent. Those in relationships such as these
come to anticipate the jerkiness. When this happens between
a child's parents, the child is caught in the middle. A child
may feel compelled to take on responsibilities that belong in
the adult world.

Challenge Two: Punishment versus Forgiveness

In a perfect world, a couple would know about each
other's backgrounds and childhood memories before having
a baby. This alone does not guarantee a successful marriage,
but it may help ease some of the stress of parenthood. When
a couple doesn't know each other well enough before a child
is born, parenting is less likely to be a shared experience and
this can create a divide in the relationship.

Brad and I were married in our early twenties after living
together for two and one half years. We considered ourselves
to be "headed in the right direction" when we graduated
from college. My first job out of nursing school was in a pedi-
atrician's office. My job entailed teaching new parents how
to care for their newborns. To say my biological clock was
ticking is an understatement. I desperately wanted a child.

I was barely one year out of nursing school when my daughter was born. She was the first grandchild on both sides of the family and was adored everywhere she went. When she was eighteen months old, I had a "just this once without birth control will be okay" moment. Oops, I was pregnant. Now we had to have a bigger home and bought a townhouse farther out of town. We were settled in our new home when I was about eight months pregnant.

Two weeks before my due date, I was sitting in my new living room on a Friday morning and felt some very intense fetal movement. What I did not know at the time was that my baby was in distress because his umbilical cord was wrapped tightly around his neck. A visit to my obstetrician confirmed my worst fear. My son was dead.

This happened more than twenty years ago and my doctors sent me home telling me that nature would take its course. It did not. When Brad and I headed to the hospital that next Monday morning, we still had not told our parents what had happened. I did not want my mom and dad in the waiting room while I was in labor. I wanted to spare them that for as long as possible.

As it became time for me to deliver my son, Brad did not want to accompany me to the delivery room. I had no earthly need to have to worry about Brad's mental state as well as my own. So I bravely went in alone. Every mother can tell you about the special bond she has with her child during pregnancy. For me, it was all I had. My baby's death was also particularly poignant for me because this was the first significant loss I experienced. I had no idea what grieving entailed even though I had studied the concept in nursing school. Brad was more familiar with grief. His father died of a massive heart attack two weeks before his high school graduation.

I went through all the predictable phases of grief after my son died. I could intellectualize what I was going through, but I had no idea how I was supposed to feel. Brad was also grieving. But we did not share any of this with each other. Almost everyone focused on me as if Brad had not lost as much as I had. As a couple, we had no idea what to do for each other because we had no idea what to do for ourselves.

Had I known that seventy-five percent of all marriages end in divorce after the death of a child, we might have gotten some professional counseling. But instead, Brad and I decided the following year that we should have another child. I suspect we thought it might bring us back together, but that rarely works. There has to be a strong enough connection between a man and woman that is separate from their children. We did not have that in our marriage. Maybe we never had it at all.

When my precious second daughter was born, I finally began to heal. But it was too late for my marriage. Before she reached five months of age, Brad and I separated because he was having an extramarital affair with his new secretary. There was part of me that was relieved to be rid of him. He was conducting himself as if I shouldn't find anything unusual about his behavior. He came home late again the night after confessing his affair to me and found his belongings on our front porch. He left his eighty-five pound dog behind and placed an ad in the Washington Post offering his pedigreed doberman pinscher *free* to the right home. He used my home number as the contact without informing me what was happening. What a jerk!

I knew Brad would help to provide for his children, and I had a flexible career working as a nurse. I did not work full time or move the girls from their home during my five years as a single mother. This created financial hardship for Brad and me. My girls still saw their father regularly and I encouraged this. I do not have to tell you what can happen to girls who are estranged from their fathers. I did not want my daughters to ever compromise themselves in order to gain the attention of a father figure.

Challenge Three: Indiscretion versus Patience

It didn't initially bother me that I was being pushed aside for another woman. I had no desire to "fight" for my husband; a man I now knew was capable of starting an affair while his wife was at home caring for a new baby. His new girlfriend became involved in my family because she and Brad gave each other permission to do so. I became an outsider in my own marriage as soon as that happened.

Resentment did creep in when I understood I was being rejected. I felt betrayed, but not particularly desirous of making my marriage work. I grasped that the emotional work to be done was monumental. What I did not realize was that divorce is no easier than working to save a marriage. I would have to work just as hard to pick up the pieces of my life, while also being the kind of mother my children deserved. Of course, both members of a couple have to be committed to repairing a marriage, and while Brad said he wanted to come home, he was unable or unwilling to end his affair.

I was beginning to understand that I did not want to be married to someone who treated me as Brad did. This is the basis for the divorced parents' challenge: *moving right* past my own issues and acting in ways that kept my children's best interest at heart. I did end up a better person because of the challenges presented to me. But, it was not easy. I worked at welcoming anyone who wanted to care about my children into their lives. This meant accepting Brad's girlfriend as a participant in my daughters' lives. Brad expected me to be devastated when he told me she was pregnant with his child. I wasn't.

Challenge Four: Dishonesty versus Integrity

I have a strong belief that children can be told the truth in ways that respect their needs, so Brad's affair was never a secret. We told our four-year-old that we could not be happy together any longer and that our love for her would never change. Our youngest, as an infant, did not have a bond with her father and it took dedication to ensure that happened. But my younger daughter has always been more troubled by the divorce. It was more difficult to give her a foundation of love because her family was in turmoil before she had taken her first breath.

When the girls reached their teenage years, they began to ask me questions about my divorce from their father. I knew I could not give Brad full blame for our divorce because I believe that each of us holds fifty percent of the responsibility for what happens in our relationships. But I also wanted my daughters to understand that Brad's infidelity was one hundred percent his decision. I wanted them to know it is okay to be imperfect and that sadness had driven their father and me apart. I softened the impact Brad's betrayal had on me because I never wanted it to look like I was blaming him. This was a powerful message because it helped my children feel less self-conscious when they made mistakes of their own.

Challenge Five: Resentment versus Loyalty

When I met Larry five years later, he was in the early stages of his own separation from his wife of twenty years. His two children were at very vulnerable ages. His son was twelve years old, the age when children begin to search for their identities and test limits. I knew he would be struggling with these issues while simultaneously seeing less of his father.

Larry's daughter was eighteen years old and in her first year of college. This is the age when young people begin to learn the value of establishing intimate relationships with those outside the family. It was also difficult because she is only ten years younger than I am. It was hard to understand what our relationship to each other should be.

Larry's divorce was also precipitated by his ex-wife's desire to start a life with someone new. I think I was able to help Larry, but I will never understand why one person feels they have a right to meddle in another person's family. If you find yourself attracted to a married man or woman, do not enter into a relationship without pondering the possible ramifications to someone other than yourself. Before you cross the line of sexual infidelity, especially if this person has a child, you need to understand that you are potentially impacting a child's life and you are not even one of his or her parents.

If you are married and unhappy enough to consider starting a relationship outside your marriage, leave before you begin to cheat your spouse. You are hurting your children when you disrespect their other parent. You owe it to them to make the break from their other parent with as much integrity as possible. That did not happen in my divorce. My ex-husband will still take a stab at me when given the chance.

Challenge Six: Resistance versus Flexibility

After Larry and I married, we moved into the house he had lived in with his ex-wife. This was my idea and it was not lost on my new husband. My concern was that if we moved too far from Larry's ex-wife, his son might not have the contact with his father that is so important for a boy of his age. It was not easy for me to live in that house, but my daughters adjusted well to the move. We lived there until my stepson left for college. By then, I had done all I could to make it my home, but it had not worked. I had to get out of that house. Larry and I bought our first home together after five years of marriage.

There were many times during those years when my daughters did not want to spend their weekends in Virginia. Brad lived an hour away so it was relatively easy to make the arrangements, but their weekends with their dad were consumed with whatever was going on in Virginia and they were often bored. They had to make sacrifices of their own because any activities they got involved in had to occur during the week. They told me numerous times they felt they were going to Virginia to "watch." They had to *move right* and I am proud to say they did so.

Brad did not participate in the day-to-day life that his daughters shared with me. He did not know their teachers or friends and rarely attended their activities. I can't count the number of times I said, "Because he's your father, that's why." My daughters sometimes found this unfair, but I didn't mind helping them learn that life is unfair at times. Brad certainly benefited from the sacrifices his daughters made, but not nearly as much as they did. They saw the different values their father and I built our lives on and this helped them decide which values were right for them.

There have been important events in my daughters' lives that were celebrated with both their father's and my family in attendance. Most of those events took place at Larry's and my home. Many people have told me how wonderful this was for my children and this is true. I hosted these events because my daughters asked me to and this meant a great deal to them. There were never uncomfortable scenes, so my girls grew up feeling a cohesive bond in their family because of the love we shared for them.

Challenge Seven: Revenge versus Satisfaction

Recently my oldest daughter married the love of her life. Brad and his wife, along with Larry and me, provided her with the wedding of her dreams. I have never seen her happier. But, my principles were acutely challenged by what Brad did and did not do. My message to divorced parents became clearer to me than ever before.

As father of the bride, Brad gave the toast, which was actually a ten-minute speech. He honored himself and his wife, and took credit for the job of raising our girls, as well as portions of the wedding that Larry and I had provided. The groom's parents had also made significant contributions to the wedding weekend, but those were ignored as well. Brad was making a "sales pitch" and I suspect that when he finished he thought he had "won" some type of competition. My family and friends were aghast. After twenty years of cooperation built on the shared love for our children, there was a divide. The only way anyone could come to my defense was to make a scene. Fortunately, that did not happen.

I know my bride was worried about my reaction to her father's message because she quickly found me afterwards to ask how Larry and I were doing. I knew why she was asking me this, but I had no intention of letting her know that I noticed anything unusual. I *moved right* so as not to do anything to add to her distress. I was able to tell her with conviction, "Sweetheart, I am better than okay." Never before has the value of placing love for a child above pettiness and competition been more evident to me.

My daughter was the most beautiful and joyous bride I have ever seen. Her wedding was a celebration worthy of the love she shares with her new husband. Everyone had a wonderful time. The event was beautiful. And while Brad's speech was powerful for me, it had little impact on anyone that evening, other than my family and friends. I believe Brad and his family got what they wanted that night: greater distance from me. But it was not necessary for Brad to treat me as if he wished I would disappear. Our connection is through our daughters and I thought he understood that. Doesn't he realize that when children are forced to choose, they always lose?

A wedding, or any other major life event for a child, should never become about their parents. Yet, how often have you heard of ex-spouses who doubt they could share the same room with each other? Does this ever have anything to do with the child? When we move away from the love we have for our child, we are presented with a challenge. Take the challenge and *move right* toward more positive emotion. Keep your issues in your world, deal with your ex-spouse honestly, and you will be taking the first step.

Later, I talked with both my children about what had happened on the night of the wedding. I wanted to make sure they understood that when two adults share a child with each other they have an obligation to each other. My newly married daughter replied, "Mom, what did you expect?" She was far less surprised by what had happened than I was. My children, like yours, will eventually know the truth about you and their other parent. Spending too much energy trying to look *better* will never accomplish that goal.

Challenge Eight: Disrespect versus Mutual Regard

My girls consider their family to include anyone connected to them by blood or marriage. There was a point, several years ago, when they could talk about having seven grandmothers. I smile whenever I think about how wonderful that would be.

If you ask my daughters whether they think I did the right thing in working to keep their families connected, they will answer a resounding, **"Yes."** If you ask me, I will tell you I would do the same again. Ask Larry, and he will tell you he wasn't too fond of the arrangement. As for Brad, I know he appreciates what he shares with his daughters, but he resents what they have with me.

I picture a world where every divorced parent works to maximize the love in his or her child's life. If I am dreaming, then I hope you can learn that if only one of you acts with this intention, you can make a difference. It will become less important who is right or wrong and more important for your child to be secure in the love of everyone who cares for him or her. Keep your eye on your child and remember that one day, your children, like mine, will be grown and you will have fewer challenges that require you to *move right*.

Children do not fail. They make mistakes. Parents also make mistakes. But we fail our children when their needs are disregarded and we fail them again if we do not work at treating every person in their life with respect. Once you commit yourself to doing the best possible job with your children, I predict you will have a greater sense of satisfaction in all aspects of your life.

Perhaps the secret to happiness is to do what you say you are going to do. So you can start by saying you will work every day to maximize the love your child has in his or her life and then work even harder to make it happen. Love is the greatest gift we give our children and divorce will never change that. Accept the challenge and *"move right."* You and your child will be happier if you do this because witnessing your child's joy is the greatest gift of all.

Notes

Chapter 1

Focus

The peacefulness we feel when we experience love is such a positive emotion that we seek it out and feel emptiness when we do not find it. The loneliness and isolation that can follow a heartbreak are in direct contrast to the joy we experience when we connect to another person on an intimate level. This happens when we completely experience the total person. When we don't experience another person completely, we are infatuated with them. This is very different from love.

Our inner experiences define our realities and no two realities can be the same. If you have siblings, you can learn more about the power of individual perspective. Ask your brother or sister about their experiences of childhood and it might sound as if you grew up in different households. If you understand that your own family members can be so different from one another, then what is to prevent your spouse (and other parent of your child) from having his or her own totally different perspective of what is happening within your family? Yet the assumption is often made that perspective between parents is shared. This assumption is arrived at because the love for the child is shared. But love and perspective are not one and the same. Each of us defines love and parenting within our own conceptual framework.

No one but you can determine what you shared with your ex-spouse in terms of love and/or infatuation. Likewise, your ex is the only one who can make that definition for himself or herself. When you realize that it does not matter how your ex-husband or ex-wife defines what happened in your marriage, you will know you are ready to move forward with your life because you will have accepted your own definition for what it is: your expression of truth. Your ex-spouse will develop his or her own interpretation of the truth and his or her definition is no less valid than your own.

Ex-spouses can become intent on convincing others that they should not be blamed for the divorce. This results in a competition between parents attempting to convince their child that one parent is better than the other. When this battle is happening, each parent becomes more concerned about "looking good" and less compassionate about the experiences of the child.

This leads to resentment that can distract us from the love we feel for our children. In doing so, we focus more on "getting even" and can lose sight of the needs of our children. In situations such as these, we hold on to our bitterness in an attempt to punish someone who has hurt us, namely our ex-spouse. But that bitterness, even when directed at an ex-spouse, hurts our children because their experience of love is interrupted when they witness animosity between their parents.

Some divorced parents take this one step further by trying to convince themselves that their child needs to be with them—and only them—to be safe and secure. The rationale often used is that a child is better off with one parent or the other because this parent, perhaps a mother, has worked to convince herself that she is the superior parent. But a child does not want to be concerned with finding fault with one parent or the other. What a child, a son perhaps, yearns for is a connection to both parents because when there are multiple adults caring for him, his sense of personal security is heightened.

This is different from keeping a child from an irresponsible, neglectful, or abusive parent. When one parent cannot be trusted, adults must intervene. But most parents have some value they can offer their child. They are usually not the monsters they are made out to be—they just lost the competition set up by their child's other parent. Your child's safety does have to be your first concern. Just make sure your concern is for your child and not for yourself.

When you punish each other, you hurt your child

Chuck has been in a custody battle with his ex-wife, Julie, for nine years. Julie wants Chuck to have minimal contact with their son Tyler and has accused him of negligent parenting. Chuck has remarried and has two small children with his new wife as well as a teenage daughter from her previous marriage. These children are thriving. Tyler has told a judge that he would like to see his father more frequently. But when the courts get involved in the custody battle of a child, nothing is ever easy or as it seems.

When Tyler is with his dad, he finishes his school day and boards the bus. He is dropped off at Chuck's house where his stepmother and her children are because he is usually spending the night. On the school days when Tyler, who is eleven years old, is with his mother, he gets on the same bus but instead of going to Chuck's home after school, he is dropped off at a day care center until Julie finishes her workday.

This child will tell anyone who listens to him that he would rather be at his father's house after school. This is certainly not what we hear from neglected children. Neglected children often want nothing more than to bring attention to their difficult lives. They can become whiny or withdrawn. Not so with Tyler. He is an active boy who enjoys fishing and camping with his father. He does well in school and has many friends—more indications that he is managing well despite his mother's determination to place him in the middle of a custody battle. Julie continues her quest to deny Chuck as much contact with Tyler as she can.

We are left to wonder why no one is doing anything to help Tyler. What might he eventually do to be heard? How will he feel about his parents ten or twenty years later? Will it matter then whom he was supposed to be with? Or will he have been forced to make an impossible decision to prefer one parent over the other? Julie does not consider that Tyler might have feelings of abandonment or wonder if his father had forgotten about him if she is successful in keeping them apart.

The next time you come across a child lost in a store or park, for instance, look at the terror in that child's eyes. Lost children are frightened because they realize that someone forgot to watch out for them. These children are traumatized by the fact that whoever was supposed to be watching forgot to look after them and might forget to come back. What happens in these circumstances is that children begin to question their worth to others. When viewed from this vantage point, Julie seems to be obsessed with keeping her son away from his father. She does not see the impact her actions might have on her son by the questions she raises about his father. If Julie *moved right,* she would understand that her obsession with punishing Chuck is adding to Tyler's discomfort about his parent's divorce. Julie needs to focus on her son's experience of her custody battle. It is likely that after she does this it will become less important to act in ways that diminish Chuck in his son's eyes.

It is also important that we assure our children about what goes on around them by consistently telling them what to expect. Children need to know what time Mom or Dad will arrive to pick them up. They will feel even more secure if they have some idea of where they will be going and who else will be there. Some children want to know what their other parent will be doing while they are visiting other family members. Ask your children what they want to know and they will tell you. This holds true no matter how old your child is.

Listening to our children is the best way we can learn about their lives. When we hear something that disturbs us, we need to speak with the adults involved. To not do so places our children in the role of messenger between parents. Who is the "grown-up" now? The child is because he or she is doing the parents' work for them.

No one can ever take your place

When parents want to possess their children, they may have a fear of being replaced in their child's life. You cannot be replaced in your child's life any more than your child can be replaced in yours. Parents who have buried a child can attest to this. These parents know that they can never replace a child who died. They might be able to have another child, but one child can never replace another.

No one loves your child as you do and your child's love for you is also special in his or her eyes. Others can offer gifts, possibly even love, but your child will not love you any less because of this. Someone else caring for your child takes nothing away from you unless you decide it does.

Barbara's sister Meg and her husband Doug had an ugly divorce. This couple's teenage daughter sided with the mother, the son with the father. Meg was always after more money for her daughter. Some of her requests were frivolous and beyond the means of anyone within the family.

Meg's son Alex had always enjoyed his time at his Aunt Barbara's house on the lake, and Barbara saw no need to make Meg's enemy her own. She extended an invitation to both Doug and Alex to spend a sunny day at her home. When Meg heard of this, she was furious. She stopped all contact with Barbara and tried to encourage other family members to align with her.

What is Alex left to think about his value to his family? His mother is asking him to pick one parent over the other. And apparently, this includes extended family as well. Meg cannot separate from Doug without making him an enemy. She wants to punish him and anyone who cares about him, including Barbara and Alex. She probably loves Alex more than she despises Doug, but she cannot see past her resentment and her son is caught in the crossfire. Everyone suffers in relationships with people who compete with others. The children suffer the most. If Meg could see the relationship as a positive, she would realize this would strengthen him and could never weaken her.

There can never be too much love

Sibling rivalry is an example of how a new family member can impact a family unit. It is a competition between siblings for their parents' attention. These children fear that if their parents love a new brother or sister, there is less love for them. As parents, we know we do not love any of our children less when we have a another child. But sibling rivalry tells us that some children don't know that.

Parental rivalry is another version of the same fear. Once divorced, parents seem concerned that when their child begins to have fond feelings for new adults in their lives, there will be less love for them. These parents will belittle other new adults in a child's life in an attempt to keep a child from developing any new affections.

Mary was curious about her children's new stepmother Elizabeth and asked numerous questions about her. Despite the answers, Mary would put a negative spin on whatever her children told her. Her ex-husband Brian seemed to be happier since meeting Elizabeth, and Mary was concerned that others would think she hadn't been as good a wife as Elizabeth was. Mary worried that her children might also end up preferring Elizabeth over her.

Mary wanted to punish Brian for his potential happiness because her self-esteem was not strong enough to experience his new marriage and subsequent happiness as a good thing for her children. In Mary's world what was good enough for her was good enough for her children. If Elizabeth was "better" in any way, then maybe she was "too good" for her children and that scared Mary. She encouraged them to reject their father's new wife and hoped they might also reject his new family.

Mary understood that children do not inherently want to accept someone new in their lives. Mary used that to her advantage. She created a wedge between her children and Elizabeth. It is sad that this woman did not feel respected enough by her children to help them welcome someone new because she was too busy thinking that Elizabeth was taking her children away. It did not take long for the children to join in with their mother and criticize Elizabeth. Mary got what she thought she wanted, and her children paid a price for that. Elizabeth was a good person and Brian was happier than ever before. But the children missed out because their mother knew more about competition than she did about compassion. Mary could not *move right*, and her children were harmed in the process.

Being critical of other adults in your child's life may indicate an insecurity in your relationship with your child. This is what happened to Mary. She resented Elizabeth's accomplishments and feared that her children might love her less if they began to care about their father's new wife. Mary did not ask herself which qualities in Elizabeth made her uncomfortable. Instead, she worried about how she would measure up against Elizabeth. Mary did not believe her children would be harmed. Mary's concern was of a different nature: it was for herself.

When considering the impact of others on your child, ask yourself what you are concerned about. If you are worried that your child might witness something disturbing, you need to talk to your child. If you are fearful that your child might encounter some odd behavior, you can help your child learn to tolerate differences. If you are concerned that someone might diminish your position in your child's life, you are trying to keep your child from a relationship due to your insecurities. You cannot give your child everything he or she needs. Your child cannot give you everything you need either.

If your ex-spouse is happier, that is wonderful for your child. When that happiness makes you bitter, then you may feel that someone else's happiness takes something away from you. This scarcity mentality is a competition that always means less love for everyone. A scarcity mentality of happiness implies that when someone else is happy, there is less happiness to go around. Scarcity mentalities imply that the only way to have something is to take it away from someone else. Everyone is robbed in these situations, and the child is robbed the most. All the love in the world takes nothing from anyone: it means more love, never less.

Do not compete with your child's other parent

When Sally was married to Ben, she did not work outside their home. After the couple separated, Sally was eager to build a new career. She decided that real estate sales might be a good fit for her. Sally was quick to tell Ben that she expected to be extremely successful and that she hoped he would be okay without her helping him with the day-to-day details of life. Sally added that she wanted to make much money and did not expect him to fare too well without her.

Sally quit her new job within a few months. She was unprepared to work weekends. Sally couldn't blame Ben for her failure; after all, he had their teenage son on weekends. Brandon had heard from his mother about how successful she would be and how his father would falter. It was almost as if Sally wanted Brandon to begin to believe that Ben was no longer necessary in their lives.

Sally resented her ex-husband's professional success. We know this because she was comparing her likelihood for success against Ben's from the first moment she began considering her new career. Sally was not saying, "I will be better than I was before." Instead, she was saying, "I will be better than you." Sally's major goal for her professional success was to make money. And she would compare her earnings with what Ben earned. All this was done because Sally was determined to no longer need Ben in any part of her life.

Sally had entered a competition with Ben. And she brought her child into the competition with her. Sally's validation came from comparing herself with her ex-husband and finding ways to be better. The result was resentment toward Ben. Sally no longer wanted to be dependent and she wanted her child to feel as she did.

If Sally had considered Brandon's feelings instead of her own, she would have understood that he would benefit from holding both parents in high regard. She would have wanted the best for her child, and this would include having as many concerned adults as possible offering guidance and support. Instead, Sally wanted Brandon to join her in the comparison of one parent with the other and have the result be that she looked better. And the goal was not to look better than before—it was to look better than Ben. Sally would benefit from deciphering her code of competition. This would open her to love and improve Brandon's relationship with his father.

Some divorced parents seem to decide that to involve an ex-spouse in the day-to-day details of a child's life is to admit a continued need for this person. It is almost as if these parents want to say, "I don't need you, and I can prove it. We are just fine without you. You can stay away." Yet it is not your needs that you are trying to meet. You are trying to meet the needs of your child. It should not matter which parent, grandparent, or trusted family friend is available to help your child.

Consider how thrilled you would feel to have a fabulously wonderful child care arrangement for your child or an ideal part-time job for your teenager. Now consider how your feelings change if that arrangement was controlled by your child's other parent instead of you. Any twinge of insecurity at the possibility indicates you are narrowing your child's world by attempting to maintain control over his or her relationship with another.

Work to form a bond with all the children in your life

Angela's mother died when she was a small child. Her father Paul remarried, and Angela and her stepmother Sharon never formed a bond. Angela spent much of her childhood alone. Paul and his wife were often out with friends. When Angela and her father had a chance to spend time together, they enjoyed playing checkers and watching TV. This didn't happen often.

Angela married Howard at a very young age. She was eager to get out of Paul's house and away from Sharon. Howard thought love meant "making" someone else happy. The couple was married for thirty-two years and had three grown children and five grandchildren before Howard told his family that he could no longer stay in the marriage. He had discovered that he couldn't "make" Angela happy because she did not believe she deserved to be loved and she was unwilling to look at the painful aspects of her childhood that might have helped her heal.

Six years had gone by, and Angela, Howard, and their children were still working at coping with the divorce. Angela frequently complained about Howard's abandonment of her. Angela's family members grew tired of her complaints and learned not to mention Howard in her presence. No one could share any joyful memories with Angela that did not focus on her.

One evening Angela was supposed to meet some friends for dinner. She canceled at the last minute because, totally unrelated to her own outing, she learned that her grown children were preparing a birthday dinner for Howard. Angela was so outraged that she did not feel able to share a meal with friends. In Angela's world, this birthday celebration was a direct betrayal of her. She could not see how she was hurting her entire family. She was obsessed with her divorce, and this left others feeling guilty because they could not openly share their lives with all of their family members.

Forgetfulness damages relationships

Forgetfulness is a typical tool people use to avoid intimacy. It is an expression of self-centeredness when the needs of others are not considered. Alienation occurs, and this can lead to withdrawal. Friendships, marriages, and family relationships deteriorate because of the neglect that leads to forgetfulness. When any family member is consistently forgetful of aspects of the lives of other people, that always results in less love. We often have to remind ourselves and others to remember the needs of everyone in our family. This is especially true for our children.

Arnie had dinner plans with his teenage son Justin. Arnie was twenty minutes late, as usual. Arnie often made others wait for him, as he was always running behind. When Arnie arrived at the restaurant, Justin was not yet there. He waited another twenty minutes. There was no answer on the telephone at his ex-wife Tess' house. After an hour, Arnie left and drove home.

Later that night, the phone rang. With some anxiety, Arnie answered. It was Tess calling to say that Justin had forgotten about the dinner plans. Arnie was unsure whether he should talk to his son about his feelings so he didn't.

Arnie paid most of Justin's living expenses by writing child support checks to Tess. He wanted to be more than a check writer in his son's life but did not know how to communicate that. What Arnie did not realize was that his habitual tardiness had caused Justin to wonder about his importance to his dad. Tess enjoyed feeling like the superior parent. She relished saying, "Your father is late again, as usual."

Tess never reminded Justin of upcoming plans with his father. She rationalized that he forgot because he didn't really need Arnie as much as he needed her. She never spoke about what might be done to improve the relationship. This deprived Justin of his father's guidance and caused Arnie to wonder if his son loved him. As Justin grew older, he became forgetful of others and tended to see his relationships from a "what's in it for me" perspective. Both parents contributed to this; Tess gloated and Arnie avoided conflict.

Accept that other caring adults can add to your child's happiness

Laurie was a practical person. She preferred a natural look and hairstyle that took little time and required minimal upkeep. She did not select clothes that were overtly sexual but still managed to be stylish and attractive and maintain a healthy lifestyle and exuberance for life.

Laurie had two daughters from her marriage to Sam. A few years after the divorce, Sam began dating someone he seemed serious about. Her girls seemed quite fond of their dad's new girlfriend. Laurie had no reason to believe that the relationship between Sam's girlfriend and the children was destructive. She understood that Sam would not be involved with anyone who might do his children harm.

Soon, Laurie's daughters began coming home from a visit to their dad's with their hair curled. Sometimes they would have a new dress on. Their smiles were beaming. These young girls enjoyed this expression of girlhood. No makeup was allowed because they were too young. But Laurie could see that her children's confidence was increased as they learned new ways to express themselves. As the years went by, it was not Laurie who taught her children to apply makeup or French braid their hair. It was the woman who would become their stepmother who showed them this side of themselves. These are lucky children. Their parents could see that there can never be too many people caring for a child. These parents *moved right,* and their children benefited from this.

If you are wondering how to start, start with a smile. A smile communicates value to another. Let your child see you smile. Let your ex-spouse see you smile. Make every effort to be pleasant to everyone who has an impact on your child. When you do, your child will see love. And most likely, your child will smile as well.

....

CHALLENGE
Obsession versus Focus

LESSON ONE
Keep your eye on the child

CHAPTER 2

Forgiveness

There is a theory of cognitive, or "thought-based," psycho-therapy that is based on the concept of blame as the basis for most emotional difficulties. This theory, one of many used by therapists, encourages individuals to take responsibility for their actions by moving away from blaming others toward personal accountability.

People caught in a cycle of blame define others as either "for me" or "against me." There are instances—rape for example—where one person has taken an inhuman advantage of another. Childhood abuses and neglect are other cases in which someone uses their power over another to inflict unforgivable pain. Victims such as these can begin to see the world as working against them. And in a sense, this is true. A child begins to feel safe again when someone intervenes by saying, "This must stop."

A child in this situation is always better off when an abusive parent can no longer hurt him or her. Often, a divorce takes place in order for this to happen. But it is not necessary to teach this child to hate an abusive parent. A child, a son perhaps who no longer has contact with his mother because his safety may be compromised, can be told, "This is not your fault." A victim of abuse or neglect, especially a child, misses out on the opportunity to learn to trust others because their trust was betrayed in a most egregious way. The blame should go where it belongs—to the adult who took unfair advantage of a child.

Therapists work with these children to help them overcome the dysfunctional thinking that led to the illogical conclusion that they are to blame for someone else's deplorable behavior. We can help kids learn to love themselves even when someone they trusted abused their trust by reinforcing loving relationships, even those we might prefer to ignore. In doing this we are helping a child rebuild trust in others.

As adults, we rely on our own inner strength to deal with life's challenges. Children do not have that inner strength until they learn they can rely on others. This reliance grows through the love and the guidance of concerned adults.

Much of the work that has to be done is to help these children understand that while they may be victims, they are not responsible for the actions of another. This is learned when the mistakes of one power-hungry monster are recognized as the fault of the adult, not the child. Healing takes place when the victims assign the aggressor the responsibility for the cruelty and in a sense forgive themselves for what was previously thought of as "my" fault.

Place responsibility where it belongs

Cindy's parents had been divorced for much of her life. Her biological father was not part of her life, and her mother Judy did not talk about him often. Cindy's impression was that the divorce had been traumatic for her mother. Cindy had few memories of what might have happened between her mom and dad. Judy had remarried several years previous, but that marriage also ended in divorce. Cindy's stepfather had stayed involved in her life and she felt part of his family.

When Cindy was a freshman in college, she began to have haunting images of a man coming into her room late at night and making sexual advances. She often woke up in a cold sweat. Her schoolwork suffered as did her sense of personal safety and security. Cindy shared her fears with her mother. It was then that Cindy learned that her biological father had abused her sexually when she was a small child. Cindy withdrew from college and entered intensive therapy to help her deal with this most disturbing of circumstances. Today, she is a successful young woman engaged to a wonderful man. But she did not get to where she is now without confronting the vicious nature of someone who was supposed to protect her.

Cindy's father lost his "rights" as a parent because of his abominable behavior. He could not be trusted because his potential for harm far outweighed any plausible positives. The hurt to Cindy, although deeply buried for a long time, found an outlet for expression in her night terrors. So although Cindy's father had not been allowed to continue his abuse, his previous actions continued to haunt his daughter until she knew what had happened to her and got the necessary help and support from others to help her heal.

This kind of abuse is such a blow to the human psyche that victims are profoundly confused as to why someone would want to hurt them in such horrific ways. This is especially true of the most innocent, the children. This should help you understand why those who abuse were often abused themselves. Once they were big enough to retaliate, they did.

Your anger is about you, not your child or your ex

Anger is a common emotion following divorce. Perhaps it is universal. The challenge is dealing with anger in such a way as to minimize pain to yourself and others. Finding ways to release your anger without inflicting pain is an indication of maturity. So we can't expect our children to release their anger in a functional way. They have not learned how. Sadly, many adults have not learned either.

Anger toward another is often a tactic that is used to justify outbursts against them. You might hear someone say, "He makes me so angry." That is impossible. No one can make you feel anything. However, it is true that some individuals can elicit certain predictable responses, and they often use that to their advantage.

Our children learn to do that when they discover they can get what they want from us by acting in certain ways. This is usually an attempt to melt our resolve by eliciting our love for them. Babies coo, toddlers hug us, school-age children try to make us laugh, and teenagers flatter us. Parents respond by connecting to the love or reexamining their position or possibly stubbornly sticking to their position. None of these reactions have anything to do with the child but everything to do with the parent.

Anger is also often used in a similar fashion after a divorce. You or your ex-spouse may use blame to validate the divorce. The message to the outside world is that an ex-wife or ex-husband "made" you so angry that you could no longer stay married. Anger is vented to convince others of the one hundred and one excuses for why the failed marriage is someone else's fault.

Phil enjoyed bachelorhood but felt it was time for him and Kelly to tie the marital knot. They had fun together, and as they approached their late thirties, many of their friends were getting married and starting to have children. Phil did not see marriage as a big change for him. He still expected to go hunting or fishing with his buddies on the weekends unless there was a big sporting event to watch on TV.

Kelly considered her marriage as the next logical step because she wanted a child. She was surprised when Phil continued to go out on weekends with his friends. She did not want to go with him, especially after learning she was pregnant with their first child. She assumed that Phil would change after the baby was born, but they never discussed this.

After Jane was born, mother and baby spent increasing amounts of time without Phil, and Kelly's frustration increased. Phil was confused because Kelly had wanted a baby and now she had one. His pride came when he deposited his paycheck. He was providing for his family as his father had. He could not understand why Kelly was so frustrated with him.

As Jane grew older, Kelly became more vocal in her criticism of Phil. She went to great lengths to get others, including her daughter, to share her negative emotions. Phil could not understand how he was good enough for Kelly to marry, to have a child with, and to pay the family bills but not good enough to be happy with.

Eventually, the couple divorced. This would seem to be what Kelly wanted, but she was angrier now than before. She blamed the breakup on Phil and used this to validate his deadbeat dad image. Her alimony and child support checks amply provided for her and Jane, yet she frequently reminded her daughter that Phil had left them both—though the father/daughter relationship improved after the divorce.

If your marriage failed as Kelly's did, you do not have to burden your child with your version of what went wrong. Instead you can accept your responsibility, learn where you might have gone wrong, and work to become a better person. Kelly and her daughter will both be happier if this happens, but it can't until Kelly accepts her decision to have a child with a man who would not be the type of father she hoped for.

If you ignore your relationships, they will fall apart

Infidelity in a marital relationship is blamed for many divorces. But while infidelity implies sexual disloyalty, cheating can occur on many different levels. We deceive our spouses whenever we are less than honest about ourselves. We dupe them again if we pretend our marriage is a priority while we are out looking for companionship elsewhere. Infidelity is always a symptom of deeper underlying issues, and it often begins with a seemingly innocent encounter that distracts us from our marriage.

Cheating on a spouse is a symptom of a diseased marriage and is often used to explain a divorce. But the marriage was sick before the cheating occurred. As soon as the marriage became less important than either spouse believed it should be, the break had already occurred. Some couples can repair the break. Others cannot.

Tom was married, and his wife Gloria was pregnant with their first child when he decided to finish his college education at the local university. He met Kate on the first night of class and was immediately attracted to her. Soon Tom and Kate were choosing seats in the classroom that allowed them to be nearer to each other.

Within three weeks, they were talking during much of the break time. After a month, they had exchanged phone numbers. After six weeks, they set up a lunch date. Tom rationalized that lunch wasn't really a date. But something was nagging him and he could think of little but his lunch date with Kate. He was already thinking about what he would say and how he would dress.

Tom knew what he was doing was outside his commitment to Gloria. He understood that it was unnecessary to have a date or share a bed to deceive a spouse. He knew he was unfaithful as soon as he allowed someone other than his wife to occupy his thoughts. He canceled the lunch date with Kate and purposely chose a seat on the other side of the room when class met the following week. He still smiled at Kate but made himself less available during class breaks.

Tom made a choice to keep his marriage his first priority. He understood his marriage was under some stress due to the pregnancy and that he would be hurting his wife if he developed feelings for someone outside their marriage. He and Gloria were excited about the baby, but there was some anxiety about becoming parents. When Tom discovered how easily it would have been for him to be distracted from his marriage, he used this to strengthen his commitment to Gloria and their new family.

Honor your commitments

An extramarital affair creates a major distraction in a marriage. There is a third person whose involvement was agreed on by only one member of the twosome. Some individuals are overcome with enough guilt about an affair to begin to act nicer toward a spouse. This is because the distraction of the affair is keeping the focus from the problems at home. It is easier to be nice to someone when you are no longer blaming him or her for your unhappiness. And the justification is often made that happiness is deserved at any cost. Even the betrayal of a spouse can become okay for those who believe they deserve happiness more than others do.

Dave was on the road a great deal due to his job. His wife Peggy understood that he would often be away for days at a time. She took care of most of the details of home, including managing the children's schedules. She was often lonely but worked at accepting this reality of her marriage and focused much of her energy on her children.

Dave had accepted his own version of reality. He had a generous expense account and was often entertaining clients late into the evenings. It was not unusual for these evenings to end with Dave and a new female acquaintance between the sheets in his hotel room. Dave rationalized that since this person meant nothing to him emotionally, he was not being disloyal to his wife or his children. In Dave's mind, "My wife will never know because she is so busy with the children."

Dave and Peggy's children were not getting a healthy picture of adult love from their parents. They felt less love than if their parents had been committed to each other, but they didn't know what they were missing. Dave rationalized that he was not hurting his children because he was out of town and they would never find out about his infidelity. Yet every time he cheated his wife, he also cheated his children of the opportunity to witness a healthy loving relationship between their parents.

Dave distracted himself from his marriage with his promiscuity. Peggy distracted herself by concentrating extensively on the children. Should Dave find himself a single man again, he might soon realize that once the one-night stand was no longer a diversion, he would feel emptiness. If the children one day realize their father betrayed their mother, they may feel betrayed by him as well.

An affair or a one-night stand can be a catalyst to bring about conflict in a marriage. There are instances of blatant extramarital affairs conducted out in the open. But once one member of a committed couple crosses the line of sexual infidelity, trust erodes. It is interesting that these affairs usually break up after the marriage does. Once the affair has the potential to be more than a distraction, the deficiencies in the relationship become apparent. There is also the realization that if a husband or wife cheated on a spouse in the past, what is to keep him or her from cheating on a future husband or wife?

It will not matter to your child who you think is at fault for your divorce

When emotionally or physically fatigued, all of us are more prone to disapproval of others. This leads to intolerance that makes us more prone to anger. Forgiveness releases anger and is a hallmark of love. It is sad that some children will experience a resignation that their divorced parents will be angry with each other. Such parents will not forgive each other for what happened in their relationship.

Contrast this with a family who values the input of each concerned member while admitting mistakes and accepting each other's faults. This can occur even after divorce. This expression of love shows everyone in the family that no one is perfect and that love survives mistakes. These families work because they communicate that no matter what happens, they respect each other.

William and Nancy had been divorced for several
years. Their marriage broke up after Nancy's father lost his
battle with cancer. Nancy felt that she was not emotionally supported by William during her father's illness. She
took this to mean that William was incapable of the type of
intimacy that was required in a marriage. Nancy believed the
divorce was more William's fault than her own. This couple's
two children, Jeremy and Susie, were school-age and lived
with their mother during the week and visited their father
most weekends. Recently, William started dating again. The
children had met his new girlfriend, Jessica, who did not
have children of her own.

Nancy started calling William to make last-minute
changes to the weekend schedule. She told him that she
worried about Jessica's influence over the kids and accused
him of letting his girlfriend get in the way of his being a
responsible father. Nancy did not like seeing William being
supportive of someone new and in the process was trying to
close their children off from his love.

In time, Nancy understood this. She recognized that her
anger was partly due to her unresolved feelings about her
father's death and her divorce. Nancy worked at separat-
ing her feelings of love for her children from her unresolved
issues. She and William worked at compromising their weekend schedules. They learned to listen to their kids because
they had learned to listen to their hearts.

In unforgiving relationships, a fatigue sets in. More
energy is going out than coming in. Parents are already
prone to this kind of exhaustion because of how much
emotional energy children drain from their parents. This is
what happened to Nancy. Her emotional energy was being
depleted by her unresolved blame and grief. She did little

to take care of herself and was emotionally and physically fatigued. She started eating healthier and exercising regularly. She treated herself with kindness. Once she became gentler with herself, she began treating others with greater kindness, including William and her two children. Nancy *moved right* when she began to understand the need to forgive William for what had happened in their marriage.

If you do not take care of yourself, your fatigue will make you more prone to anger. Your anger shows that you care enough to get worked up emotionally. And unresolved feelings about your divorce and your ex-spouse may be creating issues for you that are uncomfortable. The challenge is to learn to release the anger you feel by understanding the extent to which you are blaming others for your failed relationships. Each person in a relationship is responsible for what he or she does or does not do. When you accept yourself as an equal participant by accepting your own contribution, even if it included ignoring others and their needs, you will begin to understand intimacy on a whole new level.

If you let your children blame you, they will

When we feel misunderstood, the childish parts of us want to blame someone else. The same is true for our children. As parents, we listen to the excuses our kids make for their mistakes. Then, like children, we may also make excuses for ourselves when we do not want to accept responsibility.

When we understand that we can only control ourselves, we become less likely to blame others for our mistakes. This is the basis for teaching children to control their impulses. We tell them that they are responsible for their outbursts so it is important that we also take responsibility for our own behavior. When we say to our children, "You make me so angry," we are trying to tell our children that our anger is their fault. Yet that is impossible. Both our anger and our capacity for apologizing lie within us and only us.

After a divorce, some parents begin to blame their ex-spouse for a child's difficulties. When this happens, a child cannot learn to be responsible for himself or herself. And the parents are complicit in this. Mom blames Dad, or Dad blames Mom, and a child feels powerless over his or her life. It is true that some parents are to blame for abuse or neglect, but parents compound this if they don't help their children learn to take responsibility over aspects of their life within their control, such as schoolwork and household chores. This helps children learn to rely on themselves.

A child's most convenient target when avoiding responsibility is you, the parent. If you feel guilt about your divorce, you may feel you deserve some of the blame. You are not doing your child any favors by accepting the blame. Your divorce has created a challenging situation for everyone, so all family members owe each other some measure of cooperation in making it work. If you expect your children to fall apart after your divorce, they will.

If your children blame you and you become the scapegoat, then you are teaching your children that it is unnecessary to accept the reality of their situation—namely that there is a divorce to contend with. These are the children who will blame your divorce for their personal failures. This can continue well into adulthood. This cycle of blame becomes part of the definition of the divorce and discourages children from accepting responsibility for themselves.

Blame is a distraction we use to avoid looking at aspects of ourselves that make us uncomfortable. When we decide that difficulties are someone else's fault we are making excuses for ourselves. This encourages us to be critical of others. When we hesitate to accept people as they are, the message sent is "I" am right and "you" are wrong. This is rooted in a desire to feel superior to others by elevating our perception of ourselves compared to others.

John fantasized that his parents, Tony and Janet, would reunite after their divorce. He often tried to create situations when his mom and dad would be together. This was to no avail. Both Tony and Janet remarried and were in marriages that were more fulfilling for both of them. John thought he could influence his parents if he was critical of his step-parents. Neither Tony nor Janet spoke with John about this because that would require a discussion of the divorce. These parents were not comfortable with the possible raw emotions that might surface.

Communication between John and his parents continued to erode. John told his parents that the divorce had ruined his life. Tony and Janet felt guilty and tended to give in to John's demands. What this family did not understand was that John might have had a less stressful adolescence if his parents had stayed married—but only if they also had a loving relationship with each other.

John continued to keep the focus on the divorce until he reached college. When he flunked out, he told his parents that it was because his dorm room was too noisy. Tony and Janet began to understand John's lack of personal responsibility for his actions. Had these parents understood this earlier, John might have known he needed to find a quiet place to study. But John did not tell his parents about his struggles in school because this was a family that did not talk about uncomfortable topics. No one wanted to talk about the divorce or the situation it had created for everyone.

One of the gifts a parent gives a child is that of helping him or her learn to deal with all that is not ideal. You can help your child do this if you are married or divorced. The goal is to help your child gain an acceptance for what is not perfect in life, in others, and in themselves. This is accomplished when a child learns to forgive others as well as him- or herself.

Good parenting happens when you help your children accept the realities they are faced with. You cannot do that until you first do it for yourself. You display maturity to your child when you accept the consequences of your actions. You will become stronger in your relationships with others when you admit your mistakes, ask others for forgiveness, and forgive others when asked to do so.

....

CHALLENGE
Punishment versus Forgiveness

LESSON TWO
Blame resolves nothing

CHAPTER 3

Patience

When our children were first placed in our arms, we felt instant love. We might not have realized that our babies are not capable of returning our love until they see themselves as separate human beings. The love we experience is our own until our babies learn that "things" don't disappear just because they are no longer in the line of vision.

When a baby reaches approximately nine months of age, something known as "separation anxiety" occurs. This normal developmental milestone happens when infants learn that they are a distinct entity, apart from the parent. Prior to this, our infants consider themselves to be extensions of us. The realization of separateness is traumatic for babies despite how well they are cared for. When an eighteen-month-old looks around a corner for a toy that has rolled out of sight, you know the realization of continuity is starting to emerge.

Some children remain fearful of separation long after they learn of the permanence of objects, and this is directly related to trust. Small children can be calmed by something as simple as Mom's purse when she is away. The purse represents Mom in the same way a security blanket comforts some children. These symbols represent something familiar, and this can help lessen fear. They connect to the object as a substitute for the real thing, namely Mom.

As adults, we know that our love for another endures separation from each other. Yet we can still feel "lovesick" when we are away from someone we love. This is a form of separation anxiety which expresses itself in adulthood. These emotions are common in the early stages of a relationship because, like a child, we have to learn to trust in others to share their love.

Once we have placed trust in the love of other people, we may miss them when we are apart, but we are confident that the love continues. The same thing happens for our children when they begin to experience love. A child knows love continues when he or she understands that separateness does not mean love disappears.

The stress we experience when we feel separate from others is more innate in man than other species, but it is only a matter of degree and only when a bond of love already exists. In a perfect world, a child would have strong bonds with many concerned adults and this would lessen the anxiety of separation. Grandparents offer the wisdom of two additional generations: that of their parents plus their own. Aunts, uncles, cousins, and friends can all offer strong experiences of love. In the real world, this may not exist, especially following a divorce.

Relieve your child of the awesome responsibility of running your household

Donald was born to parents who had struggled with infertility for several years. He was not a calm baby and his mother Linda was anxious about her mothering skills. She did not want to leave Donald with anyone, not even her husband Gary.

Donald began throwing toys and swinging his fists at Linda when he was about eighteen months of age. This by itself is not unusual. Linda could have firmly put Donald in a time-out, telling him that his behavior would not be tolerated. Instead, she stopped what she was doing to give Donald the undivided attention he demanded. This blurred the boundary between parent and child, and the strain on Linda was evident. She catered to her son throughout the evening, letting Gary do little in the way of discipline or limit setting.

By the time Donald was three years old, he had been left with a baby-sitter only three or four times and he had screamed most of the time. He was almost a year old before he slept in his own room. By then Gary was sleeping in the guest room because Linda feared that his snoring would disturb the baby. This couple made no time for each other, and Donald's demands made the situation worse.

The lack of attention to Linda and Gary's relationship was starting to wear on them. Gary began to talk about getting a divorce. Linda did not want that to happen so she agreed to marital counseling; however, this presented a challenge in that Linda did not know whom she would leave Donald with.

Linda and Gary settled on a neighbor with grown children and grandchildren of her own. They would be gone for only an hour and a half and planned to have Donald sleeping so that he would not see them leave. They hoped that he might sleep the entire time they were gone.

During their initial counseling session, Linda and Gary were given an assignment from the therapist that they plan an evening away from their child. The couple became hopeful that they might be able to recapture some of the passion they once shared. But the return home verified Linda's worst fears. Donald was screaming. When he awoke to find a stranger in his house, he became hysterical. Linda, seeing the fear in his eyes, remembered the words of the therapist and the importance of her relationship with Gary as the backbone of her family's stability.

Donald continued to manipulate Linda's insecurities by acting in ways that made it difficult for her to turn her focus away from him and toward Gary. But Linda was determined to save her marriage. She began to acknowledge the importance of Donald's relationships with others and enrolled him in play groups. Linda and Gary began spending more time together. As this happened, Donald began to act with greater self-control. Love blossomed for this couple as they made their relationship a priority. They were better parents, and Donald was happier as well.

Donald and his parents needed help to understand that when children believe they are the center of the universe, they will act in ways that keep them lord and master of the house. The next time you are in a shopping mall or waiting room, listen to the way some parents talk to their children. You may hear a mother tell her children ten times that this is the last time she will ask them to behave. A telltale sign is the phrase, "I mean it." When you hear a parent repeat that phrase consider that the children have likely learned that what Mom says means nothing at all.

Perhaps such a mother has placed too much focus on her children and ignored her own needs. This places a strain on other adult relationships, even a marriage. The basis for a healthy marriage is to keep some measure of focus even when the demands of parenthood seem monumental. Children do not understand this unless we teach them that we require the companionship of other adults. Initially some children will not like this and will work to place themselves between you and others.

Children test our patience when they act in ways that distract us from our needs. As our patience wears thin, we can react impulsively and often with anger aimed at the most innocent, our children. When we *move right,* we will be considering our children's need for us to spare them the difficulties of the adult world until they are equipped to manage the challenges presented to them.

The bond with your ex-spouse affects you and your child's future

Some divorced parents continue to spend time together during holidays and vacations even after divorce. These couples, although divorced, have decided that continuing to do things as a family is important for them and their child. This often represents a sacrifice. Developing new adult relationships is already a challenge after a divorce, and this can be compounded if new partners feel threatened by the connection between ex-spouses. It has to be clear to a new love interest that the connection is through the child.

It is wonderful when divorced parents remain friends. Often this friendship is strengthened by sharing the joys of parenthood. But potential new partners need to feel a special bond with us for intimacy to develop. If this results in a healthy second marriage, the entire family benefits. The child benefits the most because he or she will see that devotion between adults strengthens everyone.

Phyllis and Cliff divorced when their daughter Andrea was three years old. Cliff made contributions to Andrea's upbringing begrudgingly because Phyllis repeatedly told him that his daughter did not want to see him. Phyllis bragged to others about the close relationship she had with her daughter and that they were best friends.

When Phyllis met a new single man, he didn't stick around for long. Once he saw the overbearing closeness of mother and daughter, the relationship fizzled out. This was fine as far as Phyllis was concerned because it gave her and Andrea plenty to talk about.

When Andrea was a senior in high school, she was offered a scholarship at an out-of-state school. Phyllis began to feel anxious as the day approached for her daughter to leave. While at the airport saying goodbye, she met Al. Soon they were together almost constantly.

Al and his ex-wife Carmen had remained friends since their divorce, even after she married Pete. They all spent time together with their two school-age children, CJ and Jenny. Al was comfortable with this arrangement. But he was unsure of how Phyllis would fit in.

As summer approached, Phyllis and Al began to talk about vacationing together and decided that a large beach house would be perfect. Different members of their families could visit at different times of the week. Andrea was attending summer school and would not be able to join them. She was relieved to have an excuse because she was tired of hearing about how wonderful Al was in bed.

Phyllis was surprised when she learned that Carmen and Pete would be joining them at the beach, along with CJ and Jenny. Phyllis was not comfortable with the link that remained with Al and Carmen although the focus was on the children. Al had wondered why Phyllis never spoke with her ex-husband, and he was beginning to understand that Phyllis and Cliff could not sustain a bond with each other even as it related to Andrea. It saddened him that this signaled the end of his relationship with Phyllis, but he was unwilling to create turmoil for Jenny and CJ for a woman who seemed to take little effort to maintain a relationship with her ex-husband that might benefit their daughter.

An unhappy marriage sends a child mixed messages about love

Kim and Stewart were considering divorce when they learned they were going to have a baby. They decided to try to make the marriage work for the sake of their child. Kim and Stewart made Kevin the center of their family and related to him and not to each other. This rarely works.

Kim and Stewart finally separated from each other when Kevin was entering middle school. In Kevin's mind, Kim and Stewart divorced because of him. He believed that if he were more "lovable," then his family would have stayed together. Kevin was "set up" by his parents to feel this way because they had stayed married because of him. The marriage had failed long before Kevin was born, but he had no way of knowing that. This innocent boy was left with the burden of his parents' divorce because the marriage would not have lasted the few short years it had if Kevin had not been born.

It is no surprise that such children feel causal in divorces that occur after a couple realizes that parenthood alone is not enough to sustain them in their relationship. Contrast this with a child born to parents who cannot be happy together but openly acknowledge the love they feel for their child and work together to ensure that their child is secure in his or her parents' love. Which childhood would you prefer?

When parents stay married for the sake of their children, the children's view of love will be skewed toward the belief that they hold the family together. And in a sense they do. If these parents stay married, their children grow up in a home where they will have difficulty seeing what healthy adult love looks like. If these parents divorce, their children may be forced to ask themselves what they might have done differently to hold their family together.

After a divorce, you may experience new love that will show your child what a committed adult relationship looks like. If you also maintain enough of a connection with your child's other parent, your child will learn that the bond a child provides between parents is stronger than whatever precipitated the divorce.

Some children will try to sabotage their parents' relationships

Sex sells. And expressions of sexuality are everywhere. Our culture is "sexualizing" young people at earlier ages. Divorced parents have an added obligation to their children to ensure that their own sexuality doesn't add to what society is already bombarding on all of us.

After a divorce some parents are eager—even anxious—to rebuild their lives. They can become obsessed at the expense of their child. New friends, dating, and time spent away from a child all create questions. Once you become sexually intimate with someone, your obligation increases. As an adult you have a right to meet your sexual needs but not at the expense of your child. If you decide that a romp in the hay is just what you need, spare your child this realization despite his or her age. When you begin to develop a serious relationship, you still need to tread lightly. Your child does not need to meet every one of your new friends or each person you date; there is no need to parade your life in front of your child.

Several years after Amanda's divorce, she introduced her sons Jeremy and Conrad to Will, a man she had been dating for several months. Amanda had introduced her kids to very few men because she did not want them to meet someone she was dating until she felt confident he would add something to their lives. Amanda felt that it was time to introduce these important people in her life to each other.

When Jeremy and Conrad met Will, there were some awkward moments since they were not accustomed to being in this part of Amanda's life. As the weeks and months continued, Jeremy and Conrad spent more and more time together with their mom and Will, which turned out to be quite enjoyable. When either Jeremy or Conrad misbehaved, Amanda was gentle in her discipline. Will had not yet been included in this, but he began to talk to the boys about their behavior in ways that told them that he understood that children sometimes misbehave. Amanda knew that it would take months, perhaps years, before Will could effectively discipline the children. The kids would have to take that lead from their mother, and Amanda was patient in this regard.

Will and Amanda were completely discreet about their sexual activity, as most responsible adults are. Will often spent the night at Amanda's house, even when the boys were there. They were all gradually getting used to each other and Amanda began to believe she and Will might one day marry each other.

After about six months, Jeremy and Conrad began to complain about Will. There was a litany of petty instances when they told Amanda what they didn't like about Will. Amanda understood that there was a part of her children

Chapter 3: Patience

that did not want anyone new in the family. They wanted all her love for themselves. This is not unusual for children after they have had one parent to themselves after a divorce.

Amanda knew she would not love her children less if she remarried, but her children needed her reassurance. Amanda was aware that if she allowed her children to manipulate her happiness then she would be acting in ways that made them think her happiness was unimportant and that they could run her life. It is natural for children to try to do this.

Some divorced parents fall into the trap of dismissing their happiness because a child makes having a separate life difficult by sabotaging relationships. Such children are not learning about love. Instead, they are being reinforced in the notion that their parents exist for the sole purpose of ensuring their happiness. It should not be surprising when these same parents begin to resent their own children.

Children can seem like a burden to parents if adult needs are not met. What is actually happening is that clear boundaries are not in place between parent and child. A helpful way to look at this is to consider that one eye must always be kept on the child, but that it is unnecessary for the child to always be in the line of vision. This means that when a mother, for example, has seen to her child's safety to the best of her ability, such as leaving a child with his or her responsible father, then her other eye can be focused on herself. Single parents have goals, dreams, and aspirations that are separate from and in addition to parenting. Individuals aware of this are the finest parents of all. They work at becoming the best person they can be while encouraging the same for their children.

The eyes have it

Children see life through their own eyes until they learn to experience empathy for others. You can begin helping your child to do this at a very young age. By age two or three, children become more social and they begin to interact with others. Prior to this age, a little boy, for instance, may be playing in a group of children, but he is playing alone alongside other children playing alone.

As the desire for more social interaction increases, children begin to relate to each other. If you are present, you can encourage kindness, but do not be overly alarmed if your child seems more intent on taking rather than giving. Children cannot understand what it feels like to have something taken from them until they learn what it feels like.

A child whose parents are divorced knows exactly what it feels like to have something taken away. This is one of the reasons these children act clingy with their parents. They fear more may be taken away from them. These children are expressing a fear of abandonment. This is when both parents should be called upon to reassure their child that love continues after divorce. Pick up the phone, write a letter, or find some way to let your ex-spouse know about your child's anxiety and do so in a way that encourages your ex-husband or -wife to come to the aid of your child without fear of being judged by you.

Your child's anxiety is the result of less trust and security in others and even if you see yourself as the primary parent, a fearful child is trying to tell you that he or she needs something more. Always make it more important for your child to experience love from others before attempting to solve your child's heartache all by yourself. This holds true even for the child who has a parent who continually disappoints him or her. Make sure your child understands that this behavior is the responsibility of an inconsiderate adult and that a child cannot be responsible for any of his or her parents' behavior.

A child will still love a parent who makes him or her feel sad. Talk to your child about how he or she feels and after you share your feelings, find a way to let your ex-spouse know that your child is being hurt by his or her behavior. This alone may not change anything, but if you keep your love for your child close to your heart, you will be less likely to make angry, accusatory remarks. This is difficult because the protectiveness we feel for our children makes us feel angry with those we perceive as hurtful to them.

Some parents will never accept that they hurt their children, and at some point these parents can and should move out of a child's life. But often an ex-husband or -wife needs encouragement to feel important in the life of his or her child. There is often a message sent, using the child as the messenger, that the animosity between parents overpowers all other emotion.

New love can be more satisfying, but you will have to work on it

You do not want your child to experience any new love interest of yours as a loss for them. But you cannot avoid the fact that for many children it feels like they are losing a piece of you. There is no reason for you to pretend that once you remarry, your child will have less need to experience the love that comes from his or her other parent. When you create a new family, that does not change what previously existed for your child. To ignore this fact makes it more difficult for your child to develop connections with new stepparents. The loyalty a child feels toward both parents is challenged when parents remarry and try to convince a child that a new step-parent will result in an instant happy family. Most children are uncertain of how they fit in, and a part of them fears being replaced in your life.

It is the job of a responsible parent to gently yet firmly help children find their own world which will include others in addition to you. Just as you would not want your child to choose friends who might potentially do them harm, you need not choose others to be part of your child's life that might do them harm. There should be some benefit to a child when a parent introduces him or her to someone new. Some-times that benefit might be for a parent to say, "I know you don't like him or her, but I do." This tells your children that you respect your right to make your own life and that they have the right to develop their own opinion of others that is separate from yours.

The opposite scenario happens when parents take to heart their kids' negative reactions to someone special in their lives and decide it is better if they don't date at all. If parents sacrifice their lives to focus exclusively on their child, that child can become overly dependent upon them. Actually, some parents seem to enjoy this.

When parents encourage such dependency in a child, they are hoping to remain at the forefront of his or her life. Parents do not need to be divorced for this to happen. There are plenty of parents who use their children in this manner, to validate their worth. The problem lies in the indisputable fact of nature that dictates that our children are supposed to outlive us. Who will take these parents' places then?

Your behavior will reflect your decisions about your obligation to your child and how this balances with your desire for personal freedom. And your child will be watching. When you respond to your divorce by deciding that you were so burned that you no longer need love, then you are dismissing your needs. You are, in effect, saying that you do not deserve love or happiness.

Other divorced parents act out their frustration by returning to more adolescent behavior. Either extreme shows your child how you value yourself. And over time, you may find that your child views you as you view yourself.

Truly disturbing problems arise when single parents either deny or flaunt their own sexuality. For example, if your child seems over-sexed that may be a warning sign. Young children can become flirtatious. School-age children can start to dress provocatively before they are equipped to deal with the message this sends to others. Rebellious teenagers may become sexually promiscuous. None of these scenarios requires a divorce, but the challenge is greater when you *as a single parent* are also navigating your own sexuality. Your child may come to believe it is normal to try to be an adult.

It is also a sad truth that children will become oversexed as a reaction to sexual abuses. It is one of the strongest warning signs. Talk to your child and his or her other parent and get the help of professionals when needed. Most important, do not believe for one second that sexual abuse could never happen to your child. Parents who believe this are naive about the potential risks the world presents for a child. Do not be afraid to ask your child point-blank about what goes on when you are not around. This holds true when discussing sex, drugs, and every other potential danger there might be for your child.

The Divorced Parent's Challenge

This can become more difficult after a divorce because you are living your own life, and you have to be aware that you are giving a message to your child by your behavior. Our children learn by watching us and if they see us acting irresponsibly, this usually increases their concern for us.

Find time for adult relationships

Most happily married couples will admit that finding time for making love is difficult when children are in the house. The loving couple will make dates with each other to steal away when the children are at a friend's house or otherwise occupied. These parents understand that their child does not need to be aware of their sexual lives. If this child sees his parents treat each other with loving displays of affection, he or she will see love. Yet even this child will be traumatized if he walks in on his parents during lovemaking. The rules need not be different after a divorce.

When you begin dating again, it is natural for the hope you feel to encourage you to move too quickly into new relationships. Until you become comfortable with yourself in a new relationship and with the couple it created, it is extremely difficult to be an effective parent. You or your child will try to find a way to express the discomfort. Children act out; parents get frustrated. The tension may place a strain on your new relationship. So the challenge is to balance meeting your own needs within the context of your child's world.

The intoxication of new love can shift priorities. Even the most conscientious parents can lose sight of family stability. You may risk involving your child too quickly at the start of a relationship because you may come to believe in the economy of combining your time with your child and your new lover.

Being an unattached adult building a new life while being a responsible parent is difficult. Some children will not approve of anyone if they fear they can be replaced. Others will seem to bond with everyone, especially when they are lonely or seeking approval. Your child's reaction to your new friends will tell you how separate or connected he or she feels and should serve as a guide to help you gauge how well your child is adjusting to life after the divorce.

If you are drawn to someone who does not seem to have your child's best interests at heart, keep that person out of your child's life. When you have met someone wonderful, be a couple before you try to be a family. And remember, your child is watching and learning. His or her questions can be answered without you having to say a word.

....

CHALLENGE
Indiscretion versus Patience

LESSON THREE
Maintain boundaries

CHAPTER 4

Integrity

One of the most painful aspects of many divorces is deciding how, what, and when to tell the children. Initially, most parents try to minimize a child's pain. This may lead to withholding parts of the story. This can be a good decision when there are aspects of the divorce that exist solely in the adult world. It is the way it is done that indicates whose needs are being served.

The age of a child should be a guideline but cannot be used as an excuse to deceive children. Children can be spared the adult details and still be told the truth. The simple statement, "We couldn't be happy together anymore," speaks volumes. Adding that this unhappiness has nothing to do with a child says even more.

When a husband and wife decide to divorce, they may want to protect their children and spare them trauma. At the same time, they know they owe the kids some explanation as to why they cannot stay married. When told of an upcoming divorce, a child's reaction to what he or she is told can have a profound impact on us. Most children will cry. Many will get angry. It is heartbreaking for parents to witness the emotional reaction of a child when he or she learns of a divorce.

Love never goes away

Some parents decide to tell their children that they
are divorcing because they no longer love each other. This
suggests to a child that love can go away. If you believe love
can go away, you may want to take a minute and define what
love means to you because when you tell a child that love
goes away, he or she is likely to believe you. A child might
wonder: If Mom and Dad can stop loving each other, then
what's to stop them from not loving me any more either?

Perhaps you married for reasons other than love. You
are not alone in this. People get married for many different
reasons that have little to do with love. You have seen plenty
of marriages in which it is difficult to visualize love, yet
some of these marriages will last a lifetime. Other marriages
seem ideal and still end in divorce. We can never know what
happens in someone else's home.

Belonging, dependence, self-affirmation, and pride get
tangled up with love. Love has become a generalized term.
The type of love that you can fall "out" of might not be
love at all. People say they love a certain movie, type of
food, even a car. Hate is also used in everyday conversation.
Does the haphazard use of these words do justice to their
meaning?

When Becky separated from Tammy and Karen's father
Todd, she did not want to admit to them that she had a
boyfriend. She understood that it is painful for a child when
he or she learns that one parent wants to begin a life with
someone new. Her conflict deepened when she considered
that she would see less of her girls because she would no
longer be living with them on a day-to-day basis. But she
was determined to stay involved. She decided that to be
honest from the beginning would be difficult but might help

ease transitions in the future. Becky decided that she did not want to begin living a lie with her girls but was unsure of what she would say.

After she began openly dating this new man in public, she knew it was time to talk to Tammy and Karen. She chose to tell her children that she and their father had marital difficulties that had brought them both much unhappiness. She did not want her children to believe that she thought her happiness was more important then theirs. She used language they could understand when she talked about her new relationship by telling them that some aspects of adult lives are difficult for children to understand and that nothing could ever change the love she felt for them. Becky let her children know that she loved them and that her relationship with another man would never change that. She added that she would always care about their father because of his importance in their lives.

The children were still uncomfortable with what Becky was telling them. They were living with their father and his reaction after learning Becky was leaving the family home was emotional for all of them. When the girls talked to their father, he told them he had not been happy in the marriage either but that he hoped it might improve, and that Becky thought that was impossible.

Tammy and Karen had been aware of their parents' marital difficulties. They had grown up listening to them fight. This caused both girls to worry that their parents might divorce. When the separation occurred, these children were somewhat relieved. They finally knew what was happening, and since both parents were determined to help them cope, they felt supported by their extended families as well. Todd and Becky let the girls know that they wanted happiness for everyone in the family and that they would work together to make that a reality. Both parents wanted to make sure the girls understood that when there is happiness in a family, there is always more love.

Soon this family started to heal because they all worked on the common goal of sparing Tammy and Karen from the adult world whenever possible. This was helped when Todd released his own anger at Becky and accepted the difficulties he had helped create in their marriage by ignoring his wife's needs. Several years later, Todd remarried. Todd's new wife became a day-to-day presence in the girls' lives, and Becky struggled to let her daughters know that they can and should form a bond with their new stepmother. This is never easy, but it is always in a child's best interest because children often feel disloyal when they begin to have fond feelings for a parent's new spouse. It is the job of both parents to let a child know that caring for someone new never diminishes someone else.

When you try to fool others, you are the fool

There is potential for mixed messages in all communication. Tone of voice and body language are powerful contributors to communication. You may believe you are being clear, but the message is received, filtered, and catalogued by someone with a different value system. This is why it is important to ask others whether they understand what you are saying. This is especially true with your children. Make sure to have your children explain to you what they understand about your divorce.

You might have been eager to tell someone immediately—even your child—about your impending divorce because you wanted your account of the situation to be understood fully.

This shows three things: You may have been worried that your side of the story would be misunderstood, you might place too much value in the opinions of others, or you may be over-dependent on outside approval. The degree to which this influences your behavior is an indication of how self-reliant you are.

Self-reliance comes from the strength to do what is best, not easiest. We help our children develop their own self-reliance when we build their confidence. This is helped when children feel proud of their accomplishments. That is why children respond so well to praise. Praise tells children that they are doing well. Over time they become more trusting in their behavior and therefore more self-reliant. But the praise and encouragement have to fit the behavior.

Some parents tend to falsely praise their children. These children are getting mixed messages. They also do not learn to trust their instincts if they are falsely led to believe they are doing better than they are. Often parents do this because it is easier to say "good job" than to tackle a problem head-on. But children read mixed messages better than many adults do.

Children who receive praise that is not authentic can become boastful. They likely already know they are not doing their best work and can start to "strut their stuff" because they have come to believe they are fooling the world. Children who *are* doing their best work, on the other hand, should be praised for striving for the best outcome. As parents we have to make it our intention to determine if we believe our children are putting their best effort forward. That is easier when we are also doing that for ourselves.

A wonderful place to start is to praise your child when he or she acts in ways that show you an acceptance of the divorce. Tell them you know it is difficult for them at times and that you are proud when you see them doing the best job they can. Telling a child, a son for example, that you are impressed with his behavior builds his confidence. When you are not happy with your child's behavior, harsh criticism tells a child he or she is expected to act like an adult. Before you criticize your child, ask yourself which standards you are using—those appropriate for the age of your child or those you use to judge the behavior of other adults.

Keeping secrets brings shame

Imagine a secret so shameful that you would do anything to make it go away. Bill had such a secret. He had engaged in a five-year affair with Diane, his wife Susan's boss.

When Bill confessed his affair to Susan, he felt a tremendous relief. Diane had become controlling of him and wanted him to leave Susan to start a life with her in a new city hundreds of miles away. Bill knew he had to tell Susan about Diane to make it possible to end the relationship. Bill was miserable and hoped Susan would forgive him for what he had done.

Bill was deeply ashamed and did not want his children to know about his affair with Diane. It was important to Bill that his children not realize what he had done. So he and Susan agreed not to tell them. But others in the community knew what had happened. It might have been a secret to the children at that time, but their lives were surrounded by others who knew.

Four years later, Bill and Susan's marriage ended when Bill wanted to start another affair—not with his previous lover, but with Stephanie. Stephanie did not want to consummate her relationship with Bill while he was still living with

Susan. When Bill told Susan he wanted to be with Stephanie, Susan felt relief. She had not been happy since learning of Bill's first affair.

Bill decided that Stephanie did not need to know about his affair with Diane. Bill wanted to make sure Stephanie believed he would never cheat on her. He was frightened to tell his secret because it would reveal him to be an unfaithful husband and someone different from how he wanted to appear to Stephanie. Bill rationalized that his affair had happened almost five years ago and was in the past. When Bill and Stephanie married, he felt that his secret was finally safe.

Withholding this significant event of his past cheated Stephanie out of knowing some very significant struggles in Bill's life. As the children grew older, Bill was less certain what they did or did not know. His secret no longer felt safe when he was with them. His biggest fear was that Stephanie would reject him if she found out about Diane. Had Bill been honest with her from the beginning, he would have been able to discuss the situation and eventually talk to his children about what had happened. Instead, he saw less and less of his kids because he could not risk that the affair might somehow leak out in front of his new wife. Bill paid a huge price for his dishonesty. His children felt excluded from his life and this added to Bill's feelings of shame. This also meant that Bill did not have to apologize to his children for his betrayal of their mother and the impact this had on their family.

Motivations for lying vary according to your value system. The little white lie that doesn't harm anyone may seem okay to some, but not to others. When your boss calls the house and you ask your child to say you are not home, or when you call your child's school to say he or she is sick because a homework assignment is not done, you are teaching your child to lie. You have found a way to convince yourself that you are lying for a good reason. But lying implies secrets. There will always be some fear about getting caught. The fabrications that are built to support a lie can become bigger than the secret itself.

When people tell a lie, they are in a sense saying, "I can decide for you what you need to know." In the initial stages of a lie, the liar feels as if he or she has gotten away with something. The longer the secret is kept, the more trepidation the fibber feels. Fear of being discovered in a falsehood can make a person act controlling and bossy. These behaviors are an attempt to distract from the discovery of truth. Liars do not want to admit mistakes because this weakness makes them feel vulnerable. What they dread most of all is being found out. They begin to act in all sorts of ways to protect themselves.

We make a choice when presented with situations that bring about certain uncomfortable emotions in us. And being truthful is very uncomfortable in certain situations, especially those in which we have to admit our weaknesses. This can be painfully obvious when dealing with our children because we want to appear strong to them. But if we are afraid to admit our mistakes, our children may want to do the same. How you react when you catch a child in a lie teaches him or her how you value honesty. How you react when your child catches you in a lie teaches him or her even more.

Do not let your children distract you from their lies

When children tell lies, it is the consequence that follows that teaches honesty. When you tell a lie, which everyone has done, you have benefited in some way. And now, you may be keeping a secret. When caught in a lie, many people will go to great lengths to refocus the situation away from it.

When Rachel's father finally got her a car to drive to high school and back, she was thrilled. Her mom Celia offered to buy a state-of-the-art stereo system for the car. Rachel was concerned that someone would break into her car and steal her new stereo, so she wanted a portable type that could be removed when she wasn't using the car. She assured her parents that she would always lock the car but she wanted the added security that came from keeping the stereo in the house with her.

One afternoon Celia came home from work and noticed Rachel's car parked in front of the house with the windows down. Her initial reaction was one of anger. She suspected that the stereo was in the car, and she was right. Celia decided to take the stereo, hide it in a closet, and ask Rachel what had happened to her stereo.

Rachel first said she had left the stereo at her dad's house and she couldn't call because he wasn't home. Several days later, Rachel told her mother that she had picked up the stereo but had forgotten it at a friend's house. Celia knew Rachel was lying but decided that her daughter needed more time to learn her lesson. In Celia's eyes, the lesson was about teaching Rachel to take better care of her belongings.

Celia could see Rachel's growing unease and decided that enough time had lapsed. The stereo was returned with a lecture about taking care of personal belongings. The more important lesson for Rachel, however, was about lying. If Rachel had confessed that the stereo was left in her unlocked car, Celia could have decided on a consequence that reflected her daughter's lack of gratitude. But the stereo was returned, and there was no consequence for the lies themselves.

Chapter 4: Integrity

Rachel was angry with her mother for tricking her and was visibly upset. Celia thought she had done the right thing even though she had been dishonest when she took the stereo and hid it in a closet. This is one of the reasons it was difficult to focus on the lies Rachel told—because Celia had also hid the truth.

Celia felt uneasy but didn't know why, and she could sense the emotional distance between herself and her daughter. She wondered why she did not feel like the situation was resolved. This is because Rachel had been successful in keeping the focus on her mother's actions instead of her own. A telltale sign that someone is deceiving you is when he or she uses "you" statements. Rachel said to her mother, "You took the stereo and you tricked me." Celia replied, "Yes, but you lied to me." This went back and forth between mother and daughter as the focus was kept on what each of them had done "to each other" and away from admitting their deceitfulness.

An opposite scenario could be if Rachel had said, "I forgot to lock the car," and Celia could have replied, "Yes, and I want you to remember to take care of your nice things, like your stereo. Thank you for telling me the truth." In this situation Celia would not have had to hide the stereo. Instead, she could have told Rachel that the stereo would be returned in a few days, after Rachel had an opportunity to think about taking better care of her belongings.

The conversation that uses "you" statements puts the focus on others. What started out as a lesson on respect for belongings ended with a less trusting relationship between mother and daughter because lies had been told but never admitted to. Pay special attention to your discussions with your children and your ex-spouse. Start talking from your own perspective by making "I" statements. This will bring about less confrontation with others and have the added benefit for you in that you will be more honest with others and, therefore, yourself.

Do not ask your child to keep a secret for you

Love is always honest, even when the truth means accepting responsibility for something we might prefer to ignore. The irony in saying "the truth hurts" is that a lie will always hurt more than the truth. Some parents will tell their children something and add, "But don't tell Mom [or Dad], okay?" The child is now holding a secret for a parent and may have to lie to others in order to protect this secret.

When Terri's father Max lost his job, Terri knew her mom Arlene would be angry. Max had lost other jobs, and this usually meant that child support checks would be late, which always created difficulty. Max asked Terri to keep his secret and assured her that her mother did not need to know.

When the check was late, Terri initially told her mother that it was because Max had changed banks. After a few days, Terri came back to her mom and told her about Max losing his job and begged her not to reveal how she found out. Arlene would not comply with Terri's request. She called Max and expressed her disappointment in the fact that he lost his job. Nevertheless, she was furious with him for asking their daughter to lie for him.

Afterwards, Arlene thanked Terri for her honesty. She told Terri that her father should not have asked her to keep a secret for him. Arlene understood that a child does not want to disappoint a parent. Terri was trapped in a no-win situation, and her father had willingly placed her there.

Truth is subjective

Truth is based on our reality, and we build our lives around supporting this. For example, one person believes that the world is evil and will act in certain ways to verify that truth. Another person, seeing goodness and kindness, will have a different idea of truth and behave accordingly. When asked to tell the truth, we know only our own reality. It might be better to ask for an answer that is honest because honesty comes from the expression of our truth.

When children look at us and see someone who is less than honest, someone who will cheat others when the opportunity presents itself, they may also trust us less. Why would children believe we will always be honest when they witness a victorious reaction by a parent who "gets away with it"?

Mike was thrilled when he got a bigger paycheck than he was expecting. He noticed that an accounting error did not reflect time he had taken off in the previous pay period. Mike rationalized that it was his employer's mistake. His children knew what had happened. It made them nervous that their dad might get in trouble with his boss. Mike assured them that he would never get caught. The children soon forgot about the dishonesty when Mike used the money for a day at the amusement park.

Contrast this to the Carlyle family and their day at the same amusement park. All four of the children looked young for their age. When this family approached the ticket window, their oldest daughter noticed that a significant amount of money could be saved if they bought the reduced priced children's tickets. The mother, meanwhile, would have no part in such a scheme. She believed that to do this was the same as stealing from the owners of the park.

Two of the children were old enough to understand what their mother was trying to teach them. She wouldn't lie for her children under any circumstance. The children in this family grew up with a deep respect for honesty and fairness. They have accepted a saying that their father shared with them: *"Cheaters never win, and winners never cheat."* When you consider that lying cheats others of the truth and stealing cheats them out of what is rightfully theirs, what do cheaters really win other than the notion that they deserve that which belongs to someone else?

It is never too late to be honest

Marisa was seven years old and had lived with her father Ralph for the past two years. Marisa had been taken to drug houses with her mother Erin. When Marisa told Ralph about this, he knew he had to protect his daughter from being exposed to such dangerous circumstances. Marisa had not seen her mother in over a year, but no one had told her why.

Ralph was unsure of what he should tell Marisa. He did not want to talk about Erin's drug addiction because he did not want to burden Marisa with the idea that her mother was in danger. What he did not realize is that Marisa worried a great deal about many different issues and did not feel free to talk about them to anyone.

After some soul searching Ralph knew he needed to talk with Marisa about her mother's struggles with cocaine. He told her that Erin loved her but couldn't be a good mother to her at this time. He made sure to tell Marisa that she had not caused her mother's unhappiness and that some struggles were hard for a child to understand. He added that he would always care about Erin and that the whole family hoped she would be well again one day.

Ralph's motivation in his talk with Marisa was to help minimize her anxiety. He did not talk about the danger Erin might be in because that might increase her worries. He focused on his love and determination to keep his daughter safe. He knew that by being honest and talking in words that Marisa could understand she might begin to experience more security in her world. This is what happened for Marisa. She was soon talking to her father about other aspects of her life, and this helped Ralph know what he needed to do to keep his daughter safe.

It is often difficult to know what to tell a child about parts of his or her world that become entangled with adult problems. Let your child be your guide. If you ask a child, your son for example, what he wants to know he will likely tell you. When you are being sincere, it will encourage him to be more open with you.

You can do this with greater ease when you are not keeping secrets. This does not mean you should tell your child everything about your adult world. Instead, tell your child what they need to know from a foundation of love. This will almost always help a child feel safe.

Be honest with your children and about your children. And start by being honest with yourself. It is never too late to share your true self with others. When you do so, your children will be encouraged to do the same. They will grow up seeking your guidance long into adulthood because they will learn that troubles do not disappear when they are buried under the rug.

You can find a way to tell your children the truth that is respectful of their needs. The first step is to be more honest about your own strengths and weaknesses. This is a worthy goal because when we are honest with ourselves, we are more open to love. And that helps our children strive for the same thing.

....

CHALLENGE
Dishonesty versus Integrity

LESSON FOUR
Secrets destroy families

Notes

CHAPTER 5

Loyalty

If your own parents are divorced, you have experienced the issues firsthand. Your definition of family was influenced by what happened. If you are now estranged from either of your parents as a result of their divorce, you may be more tempted to create estrangement for your children. This is because patterns tend to repeat in families for generations. If your parents did not divorce, you will still have some desire to recreate some aspects of your childhood. Some aspects will be good, others less so. It is the awareness of your own childhood that can help you recognize where you might be susceptible to recreating dysfunction from your own upbringing for your child.

A fact of divorce is that you will have to do a great deal of work to recover emotionally. It is unclear whether the same amount of effort would have preserved your marriage. Maybe, but maybe not. The determination to save the marriage would need to be shared by both of you. Often, one person wants out of a marriage more than the other. Perhaps these couples had disparate levels of commitment before they married. One partner might have felt they were "settling" on a less than ideal partner, and over time this compromise began to feel like a significant sacrifice. If children have been added to this family, resentment can build between the parents and the children get caught in the middle.

We first learn of love from our parents

The ways in which our parents expressed their feelings for us created our first definition of love and influences our own capacity for intimacy. If you did not experience unconditional love, you are far from alone. If our children also do not have this experience, we lessen their future capacity for love. We can help our children when we have worked to heal ourselves.

Consider where your child was developmentally when he or she learned of your divorce. Small children may have no clear memories of life with Mom and Dad and may grow up with the notion that there is nothing odd about living apart. Once they reach school, they may have a few friends whose parents are divorced, but most children will likely still live with two parents. You might have thought everything was going smoothly for your children only to have them begin to ask what happened to your marriage or to their other parent. Often, what they really want to know is whether you loved each other or not. All children want to be the product of love.

School-age children are frequently disrupted by any change in routine. When you divorce during this time in a child's life, the disruption may wreak havoc for him or her. Make sure that school-age children are rested and well-fed and that they have time for play and expressions of imagination. This is also when children begin to learn to make decisions that reflect their interests and personalities. School-age youngsters will often talk about "what I want to do when I grow up." This is the beginning of role definition for a child, perhaps a son, and he should feel encouraged by his parents. This cannot happen if he is exhausted and burdened by the troubles of his parents.

Also watch how and what type of play your children choose when you can. Having fun is one way kids attempt to cope. Hesitate to direct the play, and your children will find some way to amuse both themselves and you. Children are often experimenting with different adult roles in these situations and are beginning to develop a sense of their own unique nature.

Teenagers, especially those in the early teen years, are particularly vulnerable to the implications of their parents' divorce. These kids are trying to establish their identity, and they begin to do this by developing deeper relationships with their peers. If parents do not present a unified front, these teens can become over-reliant on their peers for validation.

When teenagers have parents who cannot agree on an agenda for them, they will use that to their advantage. What these children are often trying to do is bring their parents together in some fashion. They inherently know that family is connected, and they want reassurance of this. When they do not receive that feeling of security, they will act in ways that will bring about some measure of continuity by acting out in potentially destructive ways in an effort to get the attention of others. Parents can help by focusing on areas of agreement and build from there. For instance, if a curfew time is negotiated, both parents should enforce this rule. If Mom decides that a clean room is required before seeing friends, Dad should do the same. When a child acts out, both parents should discuss what to do.

When acting-out happens with teenagers who are coping with divorce, the reaction of the parents helps these kids learn how individuals in the family are staying connected or growing apart. If the parents blame each other for the struggles of the child, one parent or the other becomes an excuse for the acting-out behavior. The teenager obtains more power of manipulation because now one parent can be pitted against the other. But if these parents maintain a shared devotion to their child, the antics of this teenager actually meet the desired result: that of the parents coming together in the best interest of the child.

It may not appear that teenagers are happy about the limits that parents set for them. But you do not need to be divorced for that to be the case. All teenagers will act as if they resent being told they cannot do exactly as they please. Some parents will give in. If these parents happen to be divorced, then these teenagers will be less supervised. This places them at a higher risk of finding some way to gain the attention of others.

Parents who know their teens are not happy about the divorce may become lenient so as not to put added stress on their children. This doesn't work. Teenagers will be more anxious if they are allowed to run wild. It is a challenge to remain consistent with teenagers because they continually test the limits placed on them. But the greater challenge occurs when teens get in trouble. By the teen years, some mistakes can have lifelong repercussions. It is the responsibility of the parents to make sure that doesn't happen.

Do not underestimate the importance of continuity for a teen. These kids will venture out on their own despite who is mindful of them. The most conscientious of parents will still occasionally be duped by their teenager. Less attentive parents will be tricked more often. This can lead kids to take unnecessary risks in order to gain the desired attention of a parent. A secure child, on the other hand, does not need to act in the hope of gaining recognition from others. These kids feel valued at home, and this helps them learn to control their impulses.

If you divorced when your child was in college, your young adult was faced with the added challenge of redefining *home* while also coping with the profound changes within his or her family. School breaks create questions about where to go and whom to stay with. This happens at a point when the developmental goal is to connect with others outside the family. When divorce happens during these years, parents may be unaware of how a child is adapting because these years already represent intense challenges. This can become more difficult without a strong sense of *home,* and divorce always raises questions about who will live where and with whom.

Jake's parents divorced when he was finishing high school. He attended college in another town, eight hours away by car. Neither Jake's mother nor father visited him his freshman year because of all the upheaval the divorce was creating in everyone's life. When the holidays came, Jake stayed with his dad—to the chagrin of his mother. By summer, Jake no longer wanted to come back home. That is not unusual for children nearing twenty years of age. But in Jake's case, he was not sure *where* to call home.

Jake's parents seemed to care more about which parent he stayed with than where he felt comfortable. They both confronted him about his decisions and did not help him decide what might be best for him. Jake did not talk to his parents about his sense of unease because he was trying to act like a grown-up, that is what he thought his parents expected of him. But he was beginning to feel like a less important person in both his parents' lives. His parents did not comprehend that when their son left home, home suddenly became a less familiar place because the house of Jake's childhood had been sold during the divorce. This forced an abrupt transition for Jake, from being a child to feeling forced to act like an adult.

Parents divorcing when a child is approaching adulthood can raise issues about the meaning of commitment and how it relates to developing relationships with others. Questions about the love between parents may lead young adults to have less confidence in their own ability to develop intimate relationships with others. If these kids witness the heartbreak of their parents, they may want to shield themselves from a similar outcome. Or a child may be so intent on bonding with others in an effort to *make up* for the loss that accompanies the divorce that he or she doesn't develop a sense of individuality and rushes into relationships.

It can be difficult to talk about these issues because these are some of the fundamental challenges of adulthood. Parents will be talking to their children about intimacy at a time when they may also have questions about their own capacity for love. Focusing on the love shared between parent and child is a wonderful place to start. But, be wary of the tendency to blur the boundary by relying on a child as a confidante. There will always be aspects of a divorce that exist solely in the adult world.

Other children may miss different opportunities. It will depend on the age and maturation of your child at the time of your divorce. Often these children need to "go back in time" to learn what they missed in terms of life lessons. Look at your child to see whether he or she is struggling because if so, something is missing.

There is a relationship even if it is painful

Often, the relationship our children have with our ex-spouses and their family members brings us discomfort. We may decide that we can escape such encounters by keeping our children away from that side of the family. However, if this means a child cannot see someone who cares about him or her, then our distress is hurting our child. When this happens, parents are not accepting the implications of divorce for their child.

There is no such thing as not having a relationship with a family member. The relationship exists whether it has a positive or negative impact on happiness. If a child's parent becomes estranged, it is not that this child does not have a relationship with his or her mom or dad. The truth is that the relationship is not a positive one.

Your child's pain will come if he or she believes there is less love after a divorce than there was before. We know a parent will not love a child one iota less after a divorce than he or she did before the split occurred. But some parents work to keep a child away from the other parent. This places a child in a direct confrontation because it can feel as if the pull from a mom, for instance, is pushing Dad away. Parents such as these are usually quite successful in wrenching their children out of their ex-spouse's life, and the kids, in turn, feel less love.

Do not spoil a special occasion

Steve and Bonnie's separation came just before the holidays. Bonnie had met someone new and she wanted a divorce. The couple agreed that whoever spent Thanksgiving with the children would not have them for Christmas.

Chapter 5: Loyalty

Bonnie planned to be at her mother's house for Thanksgiving dinner. Steve would spend the day with friends.

Several days before Thanksgiving Steve got a phone call from Bonnie's mother Alberta. The two talked about how difficult the divorce was on everyone in the family. Alberta told him that she was struggling to accept Bonnie's new *friend* and that Steve would always be considered a member of the family. As the conversation was coming to a close, Alberta told him she wanted to be invited to his next wedding. Steve was still having trouble believing anyone would want him, much less that he would remarry.

Steve understood that if he made a scene about Thanksgiving he might spoil the event for his boys, Chad and Aaron. He knew the kids needed to maintain loving relationships with as many adults as possible to help them cope with the divorce. He also recognized that his divorce would create as many questions for his children as it had for him, and he wanted to make sure that his own emotions did not get tangled up with theirs. But his anger made this difficult. He was hurt by Bonnie's rejection of him. He often called her ugly names in front of the boys. Some of Steve's tirades left the kids confused. They were not sure what he was saying about their mother.

Steve sometimes felt unable to control his verbal tirades, and he wanted to inflict some type of embarrassment on Bonnie. He told the children that their mom had cheated on him and that this made her a bad mother. This was more than Chad and Aaron wanted to hear. Steve was allowing his resentment toward Bonnie to keep him from fully experiencing the love he shared with his children.

As Steve *moved right,* he began to understand that whatever he thought about the marriage was only one side of the story. This couple learned to work together by focusing on the love they shared for their children. Steve accomplished this by learning that he did not "cause" his wife's unhappiness. The goal for these parents became one of working at happiness because happy adults make better parents who, in turn, often have happier children. This is done by keeping one eye on the child while also taking the time to pay attention to adult needs and desires and how they balance with the needs of a child. When Steve remarried several years later, Alberta was in attendance. They celebrated Steve's love together as a family, and the children were strengthened by this.

Telling children more than they can understand is ordinarily an impulsive act. Unloading unpleasant emotions onto children won't make us feel any better, no matter how honest we have been. The feeling that we have to let go of some strong, negative emotion does not mean we should share that with our kids. When we use our children to vent our emotions, we are asking them to be part of a world they are unprepared for. Instead, when we are struggling, we can admit to our children, "I am having a difficult time right now, but my love for you will never change."

Consider marriages you have witnessed that caused you to wonder whether the husband and wife detest each other. These are the couples who bicker constantly, throw each other snide looks, and roll their eyes in irritation. Even their body language reflects their hostility when they avoid eye contact and turn away from each other. Children in these families are burdened by their parents' relationship and may grow up in such a home for their entire childhood. What will they learn about love?

Chapter 5: Loyalty

Children will dump on their safest target

We are all motivated to rid ourselves of our own tension. Our children do that every day when they lash out, often at us. They will unload their emotions on us because they are testing our commitment to them. They also lash out to release their own uncomfortable emotions. But as adults, we have to do better.

When Janice's children came back to her house on Sunday nights after visiting their father Frank for the weekend, they were often tired and hungry. Janice's first reaction was anger at Frank. She decided to speak with Frank and soon the children were better rested and fed before they returned to her home. Frank added that the children rarely behaved that way when they were with him.

Despite the children's being fed and rested, they still seemed angry at Janice after a weekend with their dad. She talked with a therapist and was helped to understand that sometimes children will break down with the parent they feel safest with. They may have feared that if they were not well behaved with Frank, they might not see him. They released their negative emotions with their mother because they trusted her to never leave them. Janice helped her children understand that Frank left the marriage, not them. These children gradually learned to trust both parents, and the emotional meltdowns became less frequent.

Do not place yourself between your child and his or her other parent

Your child will spend less time, or maybe no time at all, with both parents simultaneously. One parent may relocate to a new community, perhaps hundreds or thousands of miles away. Deciding where to live is rarely a win-win situation.

Facilitating a long-distance relationship is the responsibility of both parents. If you live far from your children, you may feel left out of their lives. If your ex-spouse is not keeping you informed, that exclusion is compounded. If you are anxious about asking for more contact with your children, you are vulnerable to further exclusion. Your determination about your involvement in your children's life is important.

Sandy knew it was important for her children and her ex-husband Dan to maintain frequent contact through e-mailing and phone calls, especially when there were long gaps between visits. When the children, Patty and Tim, got in trouble at school or brought home report cards, Sandy made sure that they called Dan to inform him about what was happening in their lives. You might think that when the report card was good, the call was made promptly. That was not the case. Patty and Tim needed constant reminders.

Sandy knew she could make the call herself, but she wanted to help maintain the direct relationship between Dan and their kids. As these children grew older, it became more challenging for Dan to stay informed. Teenagers focus on their friends and after-school activities, which is normal. Thankfully, they were good kids, but Dan felt more excluded than ever.

At this point, Sandy began to make the calls to Dan herself. When Dan expressed sadness at missing Patty and Tim, Sandy told him that it was also difficult for her to spend time with them. They were building lives separate from their parents. Such separation is not easy for any parent. It can be even more difficult when a parent has not been as big a part in his kid's day-to-day life as he or she

might have liked. Fortunately, Dan did not resent Sandy
for being a more integral part of Patty and Tim's lives. This
would have been confusing to the kids because the underlying message is, "Why aren't I as important to you as your
mom is?"

We first learned something about love from our parents,
but our real teachers are our children. Our children can
help show us the way to having more love in our lives. But
we have to let them do that by sharing our love with them
openly and celebrating all the love in their lives. There can
be no doubt about this for a child. There can never be too
much love.

....

CHALLENGE
Resentment versus Loyalty

LESSON FIVE
The connection with an ex-spouse is through the child

CHAPTER 6

Flexibility

The skills learned for survival from the earliest days of man until today are often learned after a frightful scare. When survival is questioned for even one moment, there is a rush of adrenaline called the fight/flight response. The body reacts by getting ready to advance toward or retreat from the perceived threat. The bigger the threat, the stronger the response. So the lessons we learn with the greatest efficiency are often directly related to what frightens us the most.

This is why we teach our children to stay away from a hot stove. We fear the possibility that they get burned. But some children will be so curious about the heat that they will get burned anyway. They learn their lessons more quickly, but also more painfully. Thankfully some children easily learn what to avoid without having to learn the hard way. They are usually less apt to take risks of any kind. They may be safer, but they are often more frightened by what is unfamiliar to them.

Parents often use fear to teach children to be safe. We want our children to be wary of fast-moving cars, strangers, and deep water; whatever concerns us about their safety. The child less apt to take risks will more readily heed our warnings. The more brazen child will need to be watched more closely because he or she is less likely to be frightened. But when that child is frightened, it is probably of greater intensity.

It is important to ask yourself where you believe your child falls on the scale of fear and its relationship to risk-taking. If you are divorced from your child's other parent, this question is fundamental to helping you understand what your child will need from you to cope with your divorce. This is because children who are less likely to take risks are also less likely to easily manage changes in their environment. Unfamiliar situations create fear, and your kids will be in enough situations that are unfamiliar to them that some consideration about how you can help them will be beneficial for everyone.

There is also a characteristic that therapists call *learned helplessness*. This term describes the behavior of individuals who do not take initiative in solving their problems and hesitate to act for themselves. Children often act this way if they have a fear of failure. These children do not want to disappoint their parents so they hesitate to challenge themselves. These children are often criticized when they try something new and fail. Being critical of a child teaches him or her how to be helpless. Some parents may do this because it reinforces their feelings of superiority. Ultimately, these children might have lower levels of self-esteem and more fragile levels of self-confidence because they are being taught more about failure than success.

Children want to feel proud of their accomplishments because they relish knowing they have made their parents proud. But parents who consistently find fault with their children are reinforcing helplessness. Youngsters are not learning about self-sufficiency when they are continually criticized. Often parents judge the quality of a child's work using adult standards. If this happens often enough, kids will often stop trying. Simple activities such as setting the table, helping with laundry, sweeping out the garage, or completing a project build a child's self esteem. It is unimportant if a four-year-old knows that the fork goes on the left or a ten-year-old folds a shirt perfectly.

Children who feel helpless prefer to have their parents cater to their needs and solve their problems for them. If we give in to this tendency, we are not teaching our children to take care of themselves. It takes patience to let children perform a task for themselves. A tell-tale phrase is hearing children say "I can't." Children who say this too often are not learning to do things for themselves and the parents may be complicit in this by sending the message to the child that the parent always knows best. This creates a vertical parent/child relationship and is often used to keep a girl, for instance, from "getting too big for her britches." A better response would be to help that little girl succeed in what she can do and guide her through whatever she needs help with.

Some children are more easily stressed

Gina was a colicky baby and was stressed by simple outings to the market or unusual activities at home. She demanded more of her mother Katie's time and attention than her older sister Valerie had.

Gina's father Rick was not a man who was comfortable with infants, but this is not unusual. Such men need encouragement from their wives to begin to believe they can provide comfort to their children. Moms in these situations may need to sit on their hands, bite their tongues, and let their child fuss a little while Dad forms a bond with his baby. Once these dads learn that they can actually soothe their children, their confidence increases. Sadly, this did not happen for Rick. Katie was too tired at the end of her day to listen to Gina fuss when he tried to help. Katie grew impatient with Rick, and consequently, Gina did as well.

Gina was in kindergarten when her parents separated, and she became more demanding and often cried at night because she missed her father. Katie grew more frustrated and exhausted with her role as mother, and she did not know how to ask for help from Rick because she had never done it before. She began to understand the importance of a child's relationship to both parents as she realized she had discouraged Rick from bonding with Valerie and Gina. Marriages are often weakened by this. Katie and Rick's marriage was one such example.

Katie decided to try to change her patterns and begin to encourage Rick to become more involved in Valerie and Gina's lives. She called him to set up times when he could pick up the girls. When he arrived, Katie was often exhausted. She was eager for her children to go off with their father, and she wanted to scoot them out the door as quickly as possible.

Gina often cried for twenty to thirty minutes after she left with her dad and acted as if she were angry. This caused Rick to wonder if he was a good enough father for Gina. Even Valerie tried to comfort her little sister, but Rick was starting to think perhaps Gina should stay home with her mother. Katie was not supportive of this as an option. She was more certain than ever of the importance of both parents. She was aware of the difficulty of raising children, especially when doing it alone. She also knew that Gina needed help learning to adapt to changes in her surroundings. She began to encourage Gina by focusing on the love between father and daughter. Katie also made sure there were no added stresses in Gina's life on the days she would visit with her dad. This little girl was overwhelmed more easily than her older sister, and Katie was beginning to understand the importance of patience when dealing with her youngest child.

Katie and Rick both started to ease the transition for Gina by paying closer attention to her when she was moving from one home to another. They appreciated the fact that their child was stressed by abrupt change so they spent time in each other's living rooms until they sensed Gina was ready to leave. Gina still whined often, but both parents began to see that if they acted irritated with their daughter, the situation became worse.

Through patience Gina began to handle transition more easily. Fortunately, her parents grasped the situation and helped minimize contributing stresses in her environment. As time went on, Gina was less anxious in unfamiliar surroundings because her parents helped her learn to tolerate change.

Familiar doesn't necessarily feel good

Many adults, as well as children, seek out what feels familiar. People with these tendencies often marry more than once, but to individuals with similar characteristics. Sometimes these folks can't seem to find satisfying employment. They complain about their lives while doing nothing to make things better. For people like this, the familiar feels safe even if it doesn't feel good.

What these individuals are also displaying is a fear of change. They are scared of trying new behaviors. Since fear is our strongest motivation for survival, happiness can become less important than avoiding the anxiety and pain of altering a behavior because of the fear involved.

Frequently, the person who resists change also wants to hold on to the past. Therapists explain this to substance abusers who are wanting to overcome their addictions. People who abuse drugs and alcohol, even cigarettes and food, resist change. They have fallen into patterns that encourage the continuation of the status quo. The alcoholic stops drinking when he or she realizes that changing current behavior is the only way to prevent self-destruction. In essence, the alcoholic becomes frightened enough about survival to venture into unfamiliar territory. For a time, at least, it is easier to keep drinking, overeating, or using drugs than it is to fill the void when the substance is no longer there.

Contentment happens when we live by our values

We experience contentment when our behavior is in line with our values. When we are out of sync, we are unhappy. We are either acting in ways that defy our values or, likelier, we are doing what we usually do long after it has stopped working. When we attempt to change, we feel anxiety because we are uncertain about what feels unfamiliar to us. If we interpret this anxiety as an indication that we should not change, we are less likely to take the necessary steps to make our lives better. When this happens, our anxiety is serving as a warning sign that is telling us that change is not a good idea. But it is important to understand that there will be some anxiety about all changes in your life. Fear tells us to avoid potentially dangerous circumstances, while anxiety indicates what makes us uncomfortable.

These are not the same emotion although they can feel similar. Both reactions tell us to become more alert to our surroundings. Fear tells us that our safety is at risk. Anxiety tells us that we are uncomfortable, and we can use this to help us determine what may be keeping us from being happier in our lives.

Transformation is difficult because it involves the unknown, and your level of discomfort will be different at various stages of the process. All changes start with letting go, which represents an ending. There will be some measure of grief because letting go involves loss. It is important to understand your feelings about this because letting go is the first step to making change in your life. Your child also needs you to comprehend your reactions as they relate to him or her. Divorce modifies almost every level of a child's life, and as parents, we are responsible for easing the situation whenever possible.

If you or your child tend to procrastinate, change course midway, or hate saying good-bye, you are indicating a discomfort with endings. If you don't adapt well to endings you are likely to be especially angry after your divorce—even if you were miserable when married. You may also have an increased tendency to make abrupt exits when returning your children to their other parent or shoo them away quickly when your ex-spouse picks them up. If your children are also uncomfortable with endings, you may be even more likely to avoid these encounters because you do not want to witness their discomfort.

When looking at breaking old patterns, there are three basic components. The end of what used to be defines the first step. It may sound easy, but it can be difficult when a change is forced upon you without your consent. This often happens in a divorce. One member of the couple may want out of the marriage while the other hopes to make it work. The person who decides to leave the marriage has already started letting go of his or her ties to a spouse. On the other hand, the one being left will often hold on to hopes of reconciliation.

The second phase of change involves the gap. This is a time of not knowing. The gap feels like silence, and in a sense it is. This quiet time provides opportunities to stop, pause, and listen. Most important, the gap keeps us from rushing into something we think is new without considering what has already happened.

The person who initiates a divorce may already be looking ahead to what might be. The letting go might have already happened, and the separation represents an opportunity for a fresh start. But in doing so, there may be little opportunity to understand the marriage and what contributed to the end of it. This person may be eager to start a new life without experiencing the middle point of change, the gap. When this happens, there is a greater tendency to rush into something similar to what just ended. The gap is essential in understanding why a marriage failed and what should be done differently next time.

Conversely, the person who is told of an upcoming divorce and has not yet come to terms with the situation is almost thrown into the gap before letting go of the hopes and dreams that are part of every marriage. There is a sense of confusion because the first step, that of accepting the divorce, has not yet taken place. These individuals have to *let go* before they can effectively look at what happened to their marriage. Individuals who do not manage change effectively will have difficulty doing this.

There is always a feeling of helplessness when our lives are influenced by the actions of someone else. But we can't control others. The only aspect of a relationship we can control is our reactions. We can respond as we have in the past, respond differently, or not respond at all. This is a fundamental stress management technique that we can use to diffuse confrontation with others. It requires a pause in the interaction to reflect on what we did in the past that did not get us what we wanted.

When dealing with an ex-spouse this is especially powerful. When a marriage dissolves, there will still be certain expectations about how each of you will act and react. Since you already know there were aspects of the relationship that did not work, why not try a different approach? When you do this, it will feel strange because you will be acting outside of your comfort zone. The alternative is to keep acting and reacting as you always have. You will not change yourself or your relationships, and you will be no happier tomorrow than you are today.

Anticipation and hope indicate that letting go is occurring. Your life and the lives around you will start to change because you will have effectively let go of your assumptions about your marriage. As you experiment with new behaviors, you will continue to feel some unease. Do not take that to mean you should go back to your old patterns.

Many of us will think we are in a new beginning when we divorce, although changing our surroundings and not ourselves will not bring about real change in us. Change requires learning to recognize the patterns we use with others that lessen our relationships. We can begin by looking at our failed marriages. This provides an opportunity to learn why we chose our ex-spouse by asking ourselves what patterns we were repeating that were familiar to us but not necessarily capable of bringing us more happiness.

The fear of trying new behaviors is rooted in the desire to have a certain level of predictability in our lives. But, when that leads to unhappiness, it is not working. When we begin to react differently to our ex-spouses in positive ways, we will lessen difficulties for everyone involved, especially our children. And our lives can begin to change for the better when we pause before we react and ask ourselves what our intentions are.

Resist resistance

When we experience irritation with others, we are experiencing their resistance to us. Most people resist others and put obstacles in place when they sense that their goals are different from ours. We often react with frustration because we are concerned that we are not going to get what we want. You can recognize a resister because he or she changes the subject or gives unnecessary detail. A resister will give a hundred reasons why something will not work and will say that change is not possible. He or she judges others and verbally attacks them to take the focus away from the solution and back to the problem. These are the individuals who have the most difficulty letting go, and they usually don't want to see others move on with their lives either.

You may find that you recognize ways in which your ex-spouse undermines your efforts to change your life. He or she wants you to continue to act in ways that are familiar because this helps rationalize the divorce. You may be "set up" in situations that will test your determination to change yourself for the better. Pause. You still have a choice to react the same, differently, or not at all. Your decision will affect the relationship because patterns will begin to change. But do not be surprised if your ex-spouse "baits" you to act as you have in the past. Guess what? You have the choice to pause every time this happens. This challenge is made easier if you keep the needs of your child in the forefront of your mind.

When you experience a similar type of resistance from your child, consider that he or she is expressing frustration about a lack of control. Your child, a son perhaps, is trying to tell you that having a divorce forced upon him is making him feel frightened about all the other aspects of life that are outside of his control. It will be helpful if he is allowed to make some of his own decisions. If you let him feel some control over his life, he may be less resistant to what is beyond his control.

Do not burden your child with your troubles

Bruce liked schedules and timetables. He felt that his way was best because he analyzed each decision from as many angles as he could imagine. Karen, prior to becoming a mother, was content to let him make most of the decisions, but after motherhood, she was troubled by Bruce's lack of flexibility. She knew she could structure their children's day only to a certain extent.

After Bruce and Karen split up, he moved to a nearby apartment and saw the children as often as he could. When he visited, he hovered over them as they did their homework. The children were beginning to resent their father's bossiness and were not always excited to find him at the front door.

Karen had quickly discovered that she was happier without Bruce in her house. She felt freedom when she felt in charge of her own home. Bruce wanted to control others because it made him feel less insecure about aspects of his life that he couldn't control. As time went on, the kids sought out their father's advice less frequently because they knew their dad would tell them what to do. This pushed those who loved Bruce away from him, and he began to feel excluded from his children's lives. It took Bruce a few years to learn that the only person he could control was himself, and his life soon became happier as a result of this. Bruce was particularly vulnerable to the middle point of change, the gap, so he worked at making his world as predictable as possible by telling others what to do. Bruce resisted change, and this made him less flexible in all areas of his life.

You can begin to understand your own vulnerability in the gap by asking yourself how comfortable you are with silence. If you are uncomfortable, you may be vulnerable to rushing into something that is similar to what just ended, such as remarrying someone similar to the person you just divorced. The players might have changed, but you won't necessarily be happier. If, in contrast, you enjoy silence, you may be so comfortable that you don't venture out. Either way, the most important question to ask yourself is whether you are as happy as you would like to be. The answer to that question will help you determine how necessary change is in your life. Remember, uneasiness is not the same as fear. When you learn the difference, change will become less frightening.

Help your child learn to make his or her own decisions

Christopher's life was mapped out by his mother. He was involved in numerous after-school activities, and he had a part-time job. This child was rarely still. He enjoyed nearly everything in his life, but he rarely had to decide for himself what to do or how to do it. Christopher's mother did this for him.

When Christopher was a senior in high school, his mother was killed in a car accident. She had always been there, and now tragically and without warning, she was gone. Christopher was understandably devastated. He was also lost. He had no idea how to make his own decisions because his mother had directed his life. Now he was unsure of what he was supposed to be doing.

Christopher had never had the opportunity to experience the gap between one activity and the next one. He was rushed from here to there. After his mother's death, he began to experiment with risky behavior. This was due to his grief over his mother's death and to his discomfort with the lack of structure provided by his mother. Christopher continued to rush frantically from one activity to another, but now he was often in danger.

The same thing happens to some children after their parents divorce. They have never been asked to tolerate the unknown so they rush into impulsive and often risky behavior. They are begging for their parents to tell them what to expect about the impact of the divorce. When parents are honest in telling their children that some things will remain unknown for a time, the parent-child bond is strengthened because there is a sense that everyone is working together to cope as best they can. Children are calmed by this, but only when parents are firm in their insistence that each member of the family owes every other member consideration during these difficult times.

All change creates anxiety

A breakthrough occurs when we try a new behavior. No matter how positive the change, there will be some anxiety because we will be acting outside our comfort zone. Don't take this anxiety as an indication that you should stay where you are. To do that will keep you and your children from all that can be wonderful in your life.

You may find that you are content to place less emphasis on some of your personal goals so that you have more energy to help your child. When you do this, you may experience less anxiety and be able to see that you possibly were moving too fast at rebuilding your own life. Or you are avoiding change and focusing on your child because it is easier than focusing on yourself. It can be difficult to tell the difference.

How do you tell the difference between the anxiety that comes with change and the anxiety that comes from avoidance? Look for your gap. Did you spend some time learning more about who you are? Do you understand part of what happened that caused your marriage to end in divorce? Has your family started to heal? Do you like who you are better now than you did before?

When you can answer yes to some of these questions, you might be ready to start your new beginning. It won't be easy, but it is worth doing. When you accept that change is inevitable, you will become more purposeful in choosing what you do.

Start today by beginning to recognize areas in your life in which you might be tempted to avoid change. Picture in your mind how your life might be enhanced if you made a positive change. If you like what you see, start letting go. See the ending. Feel the gap. Push through the discomfort. And begin to welcome more happiness into your life.

....

CHALLENGE
Resistance versus Flexibility

LESSON SIX
The past does not dictate the future

CHAPTER 7

Satisfaction

Life has changed so much in the past fifty years that it only stands to reason that children are parented differently as well. We may be more affluent than our parents were and have a tendency to be more indulgent with our children. This is especially true when parents feel they can assuage their child's pain by offering gifts.

Life may be easier when money is plentiful, but money can also skew values toward selfish overindulgence. Greed is wanting more than is useful or necessary. Greed also implies wanting what someone else has. While your divorce probably had nothing to do with money, it can become about greed. The irony is that when payment is sought in a financial sense, it never seems to feel like anything other than revenge. All divorced parents pay something, but that has nothing to do with money.

Money can become a symbol that attempts to pay a debt that has nothing to do with currency. When your heart was broken, you may have believed that your ex-spouse could pay you something to reimburse you for your emotional investment. Money then becomes a surrogate for your peace of mind. What is lacking in your heart cannot be replaced by money. The only way to be reimbursed for emotional heartbreak is to continue the investment in others. Closing yourself off will keep you from the relationships that will help you heal.

Long division

Michelle had been divorced from Leon for five years when their daughter Beth became engaged to be married. Michelle was thrilled about the idea of planning a wedding. She wanted Beth's to be the talk of the town. She knew she could plan such a wedding, and she also knew she couldn't do much to help pay for it.

Beth was concerned from the beginning that her wedding would cause difficulties between her parents. She knew her mother would enjoy planning an event that she did not expect to pay for. Leon was happy to provide a reasonable wedding, but he was concerned that his ex-wife would be all over town committing his money without the courtesy of his consent.

Beth and Leon were on-target with their concern. Michelle wanted to go to the best designer shop in town to look for a wedding dress. She set up appointments at the finest hotels and with the most coveted photographers. It had been a long time since Beth had seen her mother so animated.

Beth did not want a large wedding; instead, she and her fiancé craved a simple affair. She wanted her dad to walk her down the aisle of a small chapel with close friends and family in attendance. She did not care about a designer gown or a fancy reception hall.

Michelle, on the other hand, had never come to terms with the vastly different standards of living that she and Leon had. Even with generous child support and alimony, money was tight for Michelle. She saw Beth's wedding as a chance to return to the same kind of affluence she had when she was married to Leon.

She was using her daughter's wedding as a vehicle to punish her ex-husband. She expected that he would work harder to make the money necessary to pay for this event. Michelle was also not thinking about Beth's wishes for a simple affair. She wanted Beth to want what she herself wanted, namely, a grand wedding. In Michelle's eyes, this lavish to-do would make her look good in the eyes of the community.

Beth was so uncomfortable that she and her fiancé decided to elope. The couple invited their closest friends to join them. Beth also invited her father, but he chose not to attend. His fear was that if Michelle learned he had been there, Beth would feel more punished by her mother, who was already disappointed over her daughter's decision to elope.

Dollars and sense

One predictable outcome of divorce is that, at least initially, two households will need to function on money that used to run one. Deciding who has it, who deserves it, and how it should be dispersed takes on a life all its own. There might be attorneys preserving their own interest in deciding how marital assets should be divided. Some divorces become about hiding money, protecting self-interest, and withholding information about money. Anger about a divorce can encourage some to decide that a way to penalize an ex-spouse is to want more money.

One parent is usually writing checks that another is cashing. The parent cashing the checks may or may not feel an obligation in return for the financial support. The parent writing the checks may have to work longer hours and therefore see less of his or her children. The sense of obligation both parents feel is an indication of the value placed on each other as individuals. Some parents take money from an ex-spouse and still deprive this person of time and information regarding a child. Others withhold checks in an attempt to punish and control. Neither scenario is in a child's best interest.

Jim's two children lived most of the week with their mother Stacy. While Jim provided a fair amount of child support, he knew that Stacy struggled each month to pay her bills. He was certain she could not afford a new car, and he was unwilling to contribute any more of his money to bail her out. In Jim's mind, Stacy's need of a safer mode of transportation was not his problem. He did not consider that his two children were traveling in an unreliable car that lacked many modern safety features.

Jim was shocked to see a new "used" car in Stacy's parking space when he picked his children up the following weekend. His immediate reaction was anger at Stacy for spending "his" money on a new car, albeit a modest one. Jim resented Stacy's new car even though it was nowhere near as nice as the car he drove every day.

Jim was not thinking of his children at any point during his reaction. If he had, he would have been relieved that his children were no longer riding around in an unsafe vehicle; instead, he could think only of his resentment at having to write alimony and child support checks. Jim liked to brag to Stacy about his luxury sedan and European vacations. He hoped this would make her regret their divorce. Jim felt Stacy deserved her financial struggles as punishment for no longer wanting to be married to him. He could not see that her struggles may cause hardship for his children. He attributed the lack of material goods as a measure of worth. In Jim's world, money equaled value and Stacy's merit went down because she did not have nice things. This made Jim feel better about no longer being married to her.

Sometimes it doesn't add up

Keith was concerned, as most parents are, when he lost his job. He would have to dip into his savings account in order to pay his child support payments to his ex-wife Monica. He was confident that he would find employment relatively quickly, but he still did not want to dip into his savings account. Monica had remarried an affluent man. She really did not need the money to feed and clothe her children, but she insisted nonetheless on prompt payment of those child support checks.

Keith did get a new job quickly. In fact, within two weeks, he had found a good job that paid slightly more than he had been making before. He was quite relieved and decided that he would ask Monica whether she would wait two weeks for her next child support check. That would ensure that Keith would not have to take the funds from his savings account.

Monica wanted no part in his plan. She told Keith that if he wanted to see his children, he had better come up with her check. Monica was using money to punish Keith. She wanted him to "pay" for their divorce. She did not see that the entire family had "paid" something already. Keith's money was a symbol of the salve she craved to relieve her pain.

When one parent has decided that the other one has to provide the money needed to feed and clothe a child, then money has become a weapon that one parent uses to punish the other. The message to the child is that one parent works for money; the other spends it. When the economic situation of each parent is vastly different, money can become a source of resentment. The child will have an idea of what his or her fair share is and feel cheated when money is withheld. This teaches a child nothing about love.

It doesn't have to be all or nothing

There is much talk today about baby boomers and the challenges of caring for elderly parents. It is more of a challenge for these adult boomers when their parents divorce and act as if the divorce will be less painful because their children are adults themselves. It also raises an interesting question about love when a couple has been married for four or five decades and then decides that there is not enough in the relationship to sustain the marriage.

Surely these couples have had difficulties in the past. The difference may lie in trying to understand regrets some people have over unrealized dreams. The marriage may become the explanation for unhappiness. Yet each member of a couple is responsible for his or her own happiness. Just as no one can "make" you angry, he or she also cannot "make" you happy.

Erin felt an obligation to take her seventy-three-year-old mother Sarah into her home when her stepfather David left over disagreements about how the family should distribute its wealth in the event of death or disability. Sarah thought that the money should be divided evenly into three shares, representing the three children in her family. Erin and her brother Jack were born during Sarah's brief first marriage.

Their biological father had not been present in their lives, and David had been the only father either of them knew.

Erin's half-sister Helen was born when Erin was ten years old and had always been her stepfather's obvious favorite. David thought that Helen should get half of the family money. Erin and Jack could not have cared less because, over the years, they had grown accustomed to the way their half-sister was overindulged. But Sarah felt equal protectiveness and love for all three of her children.

When this couple separated, David removed Sarah's name from all of his financial accounts, including credit cards. Sarah had never had bank accounts in her own name because David had always taken care of the family finances. Erin hired an attorney for her mother, but equalizing a couple's assets can be a slow process. In the meantime, the only money Sarah was receiving was a small check from Social Security. She did not want to sell the family home because she held hope for reconciliation with David.

David was acting as if he wanted all the family money for himself and his one biological daughter. He stopped speaking to Sarah, a faithful wife for forty-six years. David was spending money as fast as he could. It seemed as if he wanted to make sure there would be little left over in the event of his death. Helen saw her father's gifts to her as an indication that she was more worthy of his love than Erin and Jack were. What she could not see was that the person hurt the deepest was her mother. But the money blinded Helen to this fact because she followed the cash as it took her further and further from love.

Chapter 7: Satisfaction

Give it to me

When Mark and his wife Gabby decided to divorce, he was relieved to be out of the marriage and determined to build the kind of life for himself that he dreamed of. Gabby had gained twenty pounds since the birth of their only child Jeremy three years ago. She wanted to have another baby, but Mark thought she should lose her excess weight first. Gabby was quite satisfied with her physical appearance. She exercised regularly and wore a size twelve. Mark, though, wanted to be with someone he felt "looked the part." He was an up-and-coming salesman at a local software company, and he often talked about how he believed his financial success was just around the corner.

After the separation, the first thing Mark did was buy a new car. He had always wanted a foreign sports car, but Gabby had been too practical and saw such things as extravagant. Next, Mark did what he had to do to upgrade his wardrobe. He felt he needed to look sharp if he were going to attract the envious glances from others that fed his ego. Now Mark looked the part but still didn't feel the part. What Mark had trouble understanding is why he did not feel happier now that he was starting to live the life of his dreams. He was going to the right dance clubs, eating in the right restaurants, and vacationing at the right beaches. "Right" was Mark's definition of what it would take to get him what he craved, the attention and admiration of others.

Meanwhile, Gabby was revamping her own life. She was relieved to no longer be judged on her appearance. She began to pay closer attention to her desire for love and affection and worked at rebuilding her relationships with family and friends. Her glow seemed to be emanating from within as she expanded her social network and began applying herself at work. Jeremy seemed to be handling his parents' separation relatively well. He saw his dad once or twice a week. This did not seem unusual to this toddler because he and his father had spent very little time together.

Gabby and Mark had both wanted children when Jeremy was born. Now that the couple was separated Gabby began to understand that having a family with Mark would have meant keeping the focus on a superficial level. She understood that she wanted more warmth in her relationships and therefore began to behave with greater sensitivity toward others.

Mark was living his own version of life and was accumulating a great deal of debt in the process. When the creditors started checking up, they called the last permanent address Mark had, that of his soon-to-be-ex-wife, Gabby. Her name was still on the credit cards so she was legally responsible for Mark's debt. Gabby had wondered where Mark's funds were coming from and assumed that he had finally started to earn the income he desired.

The date for the final divorce decree finally arrived. This couple's assets were split in half. When Mark got his half of the settlement, he used it to pay off the credit cards. He had to sell his sports car and buy a used sedan.

Mark learned that pretending to have money doesn't buy much. You need to build your life from the ground up by focusing on what lies beyond the seduction of money. Accepting responsibility for money and relationships is an excellent starting point. Mark began to realize how he had let appearances overpower substance. He wondered if Gabby's definition of happiness was preferable to his own.

Chapter 7: Satisfaction

What do you want?

If we act frustrated when we do not get what we want, we are teaching our children to do the same. When we complain about money to our children, we are usually blaming someone for not making sure we have enough. There is nothing wrong with having nice things. There is no doubt that life is easier in some regard when money is plentiful. But if you want more money, you need to consider earning it yourself.

Jason was determined to be successful. He earned a scholarship to college and began teaching high school after his graduation. His parents were proud because their son was in a noble profession. What they did not know was that teaching would not give Jason the life of wealth he wanted.

He left teaching before he was thirty years old to pursue a career in sales. He worked most of his waking hours, even on weekends. Jessica, his wife of seven years, was happy about the increased money Jason was earning. But after a while she resented the time and effort it took to earn it. She still wanted to spend lavishly on their two children and thought the family should join a local country club.

It took ten years, but the resentment Jessica felt over Jason's attention to his career poisoned their marriage. She wanted a divorce. She also wanted the money because she had gotten used to spending it. In fact, when she felt resentful, she would go shopping. In her mind the best way to punish Jason for working was to spend more money.

The divorce was ugly. Jason did not mind that Jessica would get half of their current marital assets, including his pension. What troubled him was that his wife wanted a divorce and a continued well-to-do lifestyle. She wanted no part of his heart but at least half of his wallet till death they did part.

The divorce settlement was fair in the eyes of the court. Jason provided alimony and child support, but Jessica remained resentful of his wealth when she could no longer spend as she pleased. She became obsessed about money and often complained to others that she did not have enough. She could not get over the issue of money. She had no such problem when it came to Jason. She detested him all the way to the bank.

Love is not for sale

When money becomes a weapon in a divorce, a child is often overindulged. Parents compete by using purchasing power to win a child's affection. The parent with less money may feel cheated. The parent with more money may use material things as a replacement for time. Children will brag about this or that new toy. They will look out at the world and compare their possessions with those of others. When a daughter, for example, feels cheated by a divorce and her parents are using things as a way to appease her, she will demand more and more. But worldly goods can never make up for love.

Some parents think they can ease a child's pain by giving in to demands. If parents become fixated on the child, effective discipline or reasonable limit-setting is impos-sible. Becoming concerned that a child "may not like me" indicates that a child is actually the one in charge. Adults become fixated on making a child happy by attempting to win affection through the use of purchase power.

Jerry started including his girlfriend Maxine's two children Marlene and Lindsay in some of their plans after the couple had been dating for nine months. It seemed as though the relationship was strong enough that it was time to include the children, his and hers. Jerry's children wore designer clothes and had all the latest gadgets. Maxine made better-than-average money, but her previous marriage had ended with a great deal of debt. Her children had what they needed, but not everything they wanted.

Marlene and Lindsay had never experienced the things that Jerry was able to share with his own children. Nevertheless, for all Jerry's ability to provide his kids with anything they wanted, Marlene and Lindsey were confused about him as a person. He fought with their mother constantly, and they didn't understand why he was always telling her what to do and how to behave.

The children worked to put their concerns aside and at first it was not difficult for them. Jerry took them snow skiing and to the theater, and they ate in fancy restaurants. He bought them portable electronic devices and state-of-the-art computers. After a fight with their mother, Jerry would often show up with tickets to a hot sporting event. The seats were always top-notch.

Jerry was attempting to use his money to buy the affections of Maxine's children. Jerry wanted to marry her, but she resisted. She knew deep in her heart that she did not love him, but she enjoyed sharing in special events and activities with Marlene and Lindsay. She understood that she was using Jerry to provide certain things for her children, but every time she tried to break the relationship off, he begged her to give him another chance.

Maxine knew that Jerry was manipulating everyone's affections with his money. He talked about how much he enjoyed the times when the children were included. But

Maxine had experienced enough arguments with him to know that he was often frustrated with her and the kids. Yet he persisted in trying to persuade her that what they had was special and used trips and fancy restaurants to prove his point. His first wife had left him for another man, and he did not want others in the community to think he was being "dumped" again. He could not understand why anyone would want to walk away from the "stuff" he was able to provide. He did not see that a great deal of what he provided was emotional turmoil for Maxine and her children.

The children did not abuse Jerry's tendency to use money to buy their forgiveness because they didn't have to. Jerry knew when he needed to make up to Maxine or one of her children. He never said he was sorry, but he would simply show up with some coveted item and consider the matter closed. When Maxine finally broke up with him, it was with great difficulty because he did not want to let her go. He continued to manipulate the children by sending them tickets to the ball park or the theater. His hope was that Marlene and Lindsay would pressure their mother to take him back. That was not going to happen. The children were disappointed for themselves but relieved for their mother. They had not liked watching Jerry belittle her.

I want it and I want it now

Children want instant gratification. The younger they are, the greater the desire. The infant cannot wait longer than absolutely necessary for food when he or she is hungry. Toddlers will throw a temper tantrum when they don't get what they want. If a parent consistently gives in to a child's demands, this behavior will continue to the extent that such children will always expect instant attention when they snap their fingers. They are spoiled in the sense that their inner souls are polluted with getting what they want, so they grow up to be boorish adults whom most of us go to great lengths to avoid.

There is nothing wrong about wanting all the abundance the world has to offer. It is just that the antithesis of this is to look to money as an indication of love. There is no test for love. Love will always fail when tested because whatever expectation a person places on displays of love has nothing to do with the emotion. Love, when filled with expectations about how others should behave, places judgment on them to express love to us as we expect them to. When this includes spending money or collecting gifts, we have come to define outer trappings as an indication of love. But love is warm and doesn't include cold, hard cash.

Children are particularly susceptible to the idea that whoever has the most toys wins. Some adults buy into that notion as well. Plenty of adults want nicer cars, bigger houses, fancier clothes. And it is rewarding to succeed. Earning what you want is satisfying. Being given what you want rarely elicits that same sense of accomplishment. Do not deprive your child of the opportunity to work toward his or her goals.

It is a fallacy that time is money. Making money takes time. How ironic that more of our time is consumed so that we can buy more stuff. Goodies can never make up for time and attention, and no amount of money can change that.

．．．．．．．．．．．．．．．．．．．．

CHALLENGE
Revenge versus Satisfaction

LESSON
Money is not a weapon

CHAPTER 8

Mutual Regard

One of the easiest ways to help a child learn that love continues when we are away from them is to ensure that they learn
to treat their elders and other family members with respect.
When required of a child, simple respect teaches children
to be kind and considerate of others, and this will make it
easier to share love. Consider how important a thank-you
note is to most grandparents. They not only want to know a
grandchild loves them, but they also need to know this child
is thoughtful toward them.

There are many different reasons why children treat
adults with contempt. Often, they do not know any better.
No one has taught them the value of the golden rule of doing
onto others as we wish them to do unto us. Sometimes, children are rude because they have not learned to control their
impulses and they are feeling powerless over some aspect of
their lives. What these children want is for someone to be
paying close enough attention to their behavior to pull them
aside and talk to them.

Other children are angry and project their feelings onto
the adults in their lives. These are the children who are
hoping an adult will come along and solve their problems for
them. Some of these problems might require adult inter-

vention, but often children need to be encouraged to step forward and solve their problem on their own.

Disrespect hurts the feelings of others who often respond with nasty comments of their own. It is true that some rude people enjoy the power of knowing they can inflict pain on others. But often these folks are mean because someone has been unkind to them. If your child is mouthy, your first step should be to listen to how you speak to your child. If you are quick to snap at your child or criticize him or her, your child's confidence will erode over time. As this continues, your child will be rude to others in an attempt to feel superior to them. Sadly, this does nothing to increase your child's opinion of who he or she is. It encourages disrespectful behavior toward others, including you.

Children do not inherently believe that respect is required because they believe the world revolves around them. That is why we have to teach them this concept. Kids want their parents' lives to revolve around them because the world can seem scary to youngsters. They need to believe they are terribly important to us. Naturally, we tell our sons and daughters this all the time. But if we tolerate disdain and scorn from them, we are telling our children that as their parents, we are not important. The message sent is that children are more deserving of respect than adults. This feeds their idea that they are the center of the universe. If you allow your children to disregard other adults, look out. You might be next.

This is especially true if you are divorced or remarried, and you allow your kids to treat their other parent or stepparent with disrespect. What they learn from this is that it is not important that adults are treated courteously. Such children mouth off to adults if they have come to the conclusion that someone is not deserving of simple courtesy, and they often learn this from their most powerful teachers, us. They are learning that adults exist for the sole purpose of meeting their needs. When these adults do not devote themselves to meeting the selfish needs of that child, he or she will be angry and the cycle continues. The adult begins to feel taken for granted while the child expects to be catered to regardless of the circumstances.

This is often compounded in divorce when the parents of a child have lost respect for each other and one or the other parent encourages this. It is part of the cycle of blame, competition, and resentment that many divorced parents carry for their ex-spouses, often years after a divorce is final. It may continue long after a child is grown. Children raised in this type of environment have had to accept that their parents have an aversion to each other. Instead of showing it continually, parents like this would do their child a service by maintaining enough respect for each other to honor the love they share for their child. But a parent who wants to look superior feels vindicated when a child treats his or her other parent with disapproval. In instances such as these, the child loses the most, because he or she is learning to be inconsiderate of someone who loves him or her.

Do not test your child's loyalty to you

The child within all of us wants to believe that our parents love us. The parent in each of us knows this to be true. Yet when divorces occur in the life of a child and parents act cruel toward each other, a child watches one parent hurt the other. A daughter, for instance, feels protective and frightened simultaneously. This teaches a child nothing about love as she has to decide how best to protect her parents from each other.

Perhaps this represents the biggest challenge after divorce because our personal hurt makes us want to strike out at those we believe are behind our emotional pain. Children are often caught in the middle of these types of divorces because they may feel forced to choose sides. Some parents actually enjoy watching their child mistreat his or her other parent.

A child's anger can be compounded after a divorce when parents are threatened that a child may end up preferring one parent over the other. This compromises discipline. But some divorced parents don't seem to realize this. How often have you seen vindictive parents hesitate to set limits with their child because they are concerned that the child will go to the home with the fewest rules?

A child will feel less compelled to listen to a parent who is treated as not deserving of respect by his or her other parent. The end result may be the manipulation of one parent against the other. Every child will attempt to do this. But when there are two households with differing agendas, a child can more easily pit one parent against the other.

Lose the focus, lose the child

Emily was a teenager when her parents, Joe and Betsy, split up. Both parents remarried within a relatively short time. Joe and Betsy did not talk to each other about Emily unless they saw a problem. Emily was skilled at being sneaky, so her parents did not see that their child was in trouble.

Emily quickly learned that she could tell one parent one story and the other parent another story. She knew that Joe and Betsy would not compare stories or check on her as she moved from one parent's home to the other. This often left

Emily without any adult supervision—each of her parents
assumed the other was in charge. This was exacerbated by
the fact that Emily was unhappy about her parent's divorce.
She was unpleasant to have around, and her parents were
often relieved to have her somewhere other than with them.

Emily was making a cry for help when she began to
abuse drugs and alcohol. She also was often sexually promiscuous, especially after a night of heavy drinking. She was
engaging in risk-taking behaviors in hopes of getting her
parents' attention. It didn't work. Joe and Betsy remained
clueless about their daughter's alcohol and drug abuse
because they rarely discussed her with each other.

Emily was angry with her parents, but she was taking her
anger out on herself. She knew she was headed for trouble,
but in her immature mind this is what her parents deserved.
She felt excluded from her parents' lives and, in response
to this, decided she would teach them a lesson by sneaking
around and abusing her body. In effect, this child was saying,
"I'll show you that you don't know what you are doing."

Emily would have been better served if Joe and Betsy
had kept an open dialogue about what was going on with
her. But these parents had taken their eyes off their child.
They wanted new and improved love in their lives after the
divorce. This translated into less attention being given to
Emily. Love can never be new or improved. We can't love
someone a little bit. With love, it is all or nothing.

Emily would have been happy with any of the old love
she had felt before her parents divorced. But her parents had
lost sight of her needs. They had lost respect for each other
over the years, and this made it difficult for them to parent
Emily effectively. They saw no need to ensure that Emily
treated each parent with courtesy. Even less was said when

Chapter 8: Mutual Regard

Emily was nasty to one of her stepparents. This left Emily feeling unimportant to her parents, and her expressions of disregard for others increased.

Emily felt that she had lost her loving family when Joe and Betsy divorced. Yet her parents did not love her any less now than they did before. They just had too much difficulty keeping their daughter's needs a priority because they no longer cared enough for or about each other to ensure that Emily treated all her family members with courtesy. When Emily became hard to handle, these parents came to expect less from their child because they had come to expect less from themselves.

Joe and Betsy could not maintain the smallest level of esteem for one another so they taught their daughter contempt instead of honor. She learned to treat her parents and stepparents with disrespect from the most powerful teacher children have—their own parents. Lamentably, she also lost respect for herself somewhere along the way. Emily was not acting disrespectful on purpose. She was trying to tell her parents that she was in emotional pain and feeling alone.

When Emily was caught drinking at a school dance, her parents were shocked. During the required family counseling sessions Joe and Betsy were finally made aware of their daughter's struggles and began to keep a closer eye on her. Eventually, Joe and Betsy reestablished enough of a bond with each other to act with their daughter's best interest at heart. Emily began to smile more and her relationships with all the members in her family improved. This was facilitated as Emily now saw her mom and dad come together in her best interest and that meant she felt more love. Joe and Betsy *moved right* toward mutual regard for each other, and Emily learned to respect her parents because they began to treat each other with more understanding.

Finest quality or worst trait?

When a marriage ends, it doesn't mean the issues creating the divorce disappear. You have to deal with the same personality characteristics in each other now as you did before the divorce. What can start to happen is that an ex-spouse's personality characteristics get catalogued into positive and negative traits. When the relationship became less than fulfilling, the negative traits seemed more predominant. More likely, it is the perception that changed how the characteristic was defined.

Whatever type of parent you were before your divorce, you are likely to be an exaggeration of that in the initial stages after your divorce. If you were controlling, you may become more so. If you were permissive, that will continue as well. A child quickly learns how to play one parent off the other and will act accordingly. That is a hallmark of childhood—trying to get what you want but not necessarily what is best.

Consider a characteristic in your child that you admire. Now think about how this characteristic can also show up in your child in a negative way. This exercise has nothing to do with your child but is helpful in illustrating that our best qualities can be our worst traits. The determined child can be a perfectionist. The easygoing child might put things off until the last minute.

We also have attributes that when used effectively make us stronger but when used excessively make us vulnerable. As adults, we work to temper these extremes. We need to help our children do the same thing.

Chapter 8: Mutual Regard

After a divorce, this can get complicated. Ex-husbands also have certain characteristics that represent the best and worst in them. The characteristic itself now becomes less important than the framework in which it is viewed. When we are in touch with loving feelings toward each other, we tend to see our ex-spouse's characteristics positively. When viewed through the prism of competition and resentment, the characteristic will look totally different. But the trait is the same as it was before. The interpretation is the only thing that has changed.

If you see qualities in your child that you have come to despise in your ex-spouse, you may project your irritation at your ex-husband or ex-wife onto your child. Avoiding such unfairness is even more of a challenge when a child physically resembles an ex-husband or ex-wife. If the divorce is testy, the child may serve as a constant reminder of the person you could not stay married to. He or she becomes a symbol for failure. Yet who is failing whom in this scenario?

"You are just like your mother [father]," should be said to a child as a compliment. After all, children want to emulate aspects of their parents' behavior that they admire. Yet often, such a comment is made in anger as a way to reject a child's other parent and to shame both of them. A girl, for example, may love her other parent dearly—perhaps it's her father—and she can't understand what is so disgraceful about acting like him.

We all act from our own perspective and are interpreted by others—namely, the person we're talking to. Sometimes, our behavior is perceived by others as being rude without that being our intent at all. Other times we are expressing a deeper agony when we act mean toward others. But hurting someone else's feelings doesn't make us feel better, at least not in the long run. Negative emotions spiral down, often at astonishing speed, and drag everyone involved down as well. Positive emotions elevate us and encourage kindness and compassion. It is not surprising that levels of happiness increase when our hearts are focused on others while negative emotions almost always result in making us feel less happiness.

Check in with others before you check out

Marcia and Richard began to bicker soon after their first child was born. Marcia came from a large family where her mom and dad were clearly in charge. Individual differences were not celebrated in this nuclear family. There was an underlying concern about appearances. Marcia was from a "what will the neighbors think" family. Richard came from a home where things were fairly tense. His mother was verbally abusive, so he learned that even if he thought he was right, it would be best to stay quiet. He was from a "just keep quiet" family.

Taking charge, along with saying nothing to anger anyone, worked fine for this couple until they became parents. Marcia was in charge, and Richard avoided conflict. After their daughter Lucy was born, Marcia insisted on telling Richard how to do everything with their baby. At first Richard acquiesced.

As Lucy grew older, she became a bossy child. Marcia made excuses for this behavior by telling others that her daughter was exceptionally bright. This mother also watched her child closely in her interactions with others. When she saw Lucy allowing others to direct her play, Marcia would intervene. She did not want her daughter to be passive. She saw that characteristic in her husband and did not want to see it in her child.

Not all of Richard's agreeable nature was due to his passivity. He was a gentle man. As a child, he had learned that fighting over every detail of life created unnecessary tension in a family. Yet Marcia did not see things as Richard did. Her parents had been in charge in her household, and Marcia wanted to control her home as well.

As time went on, Richard resented being told what to do. He knew that some of his parenting decisions were good ones. It was not that he could not make decisions—it was that he was unaccustomed to asserting himself. He had learned to stay quiet to keep a potentially volatile situation from escalating.

What started to happen is that this couple began to anticipate what would happen before it took place. Richard assumed Marcia would nag him every time she opened her mouth. Marcia anticipated that Richard would not have an opinion one way or the other about the matter at hand so each time she initiated a conversation, she expected Richard was waiting to be told what to do.

In Marcia's world, Richard was just another needy person who required her direction. She was fatigued with being a mother because she did not know how to ask for support from others. As Richard withdrew emotionally from his wife, her feelings of isolation were compounded. This caused Marcia to escalate her demands, thinking that if he would just listen to her, then he would know what needed to be done. But Richard could not listen because he had begun to shield himself from his wife's domineering manner.

Authentic communication cannot occur when assumptions such as these are in place. No matter what Marcia might have been trying to say, Richard read something into her tone of voice that verified what he thought was true, that his wife was a nag. Meanwhile, she took his reticence to assert himself as an indication that he did not know what he was supposed to do. She assumed that he was waiting for her to tell him.

As this couple's irritation escalated, they consistently spoke with each other with annoyance in their voices. Body language revealed their inner feelings. This couple was rapidly losing respect for each other. Marcia no longer cared about Richard's laid-back attitude; instead she saw it as submission. As expected, he no longer respected Marcia's take-charge personality; he saw her as manipulative. Lucy was not sure who she should listen to so she spent increasing amounts of time upstairs in her bedroom or visiting friends. She wished her mom wasn't so bossy but didn't dare say so and felt pity for her father because he acted as if he were frightened by Marcia. This taught Lucy nothing about love.

When spouses respect each other, they offer the benefit of the doubt. They are willing to consider that the tone of voice or body language is not directed at them but is part of how their partner is coping with his or her day. When husbands and wives stop giving each other that benefit of the doubt, they take everything personally. They feel attacked when the situation may have nothing to do with them. You know how frazzled you have been when all you wanted from your partner was some consideration. If you felt misunderstood, you may be less likely to reach out next time. When this happens often enough, most people will simply stop asking.

This is part of what happened to Marcia and Richard. They were no longer willing to give each other the benefit of the doubt because they did not feel understood by each other. Their expectations encouraged them to believe they knew what each other was thinking and acted accordingly. The affection Richard and Marcia had for each other was getting buried underneath their assumptions. This couple may be able to repair the break that is occurring in their marriage, but it will require kindness, respect, and consideration for each other's feelings. In doing this, this couple will also be teaching Lucy about love.

Asking others for support is a strength, not a weakness

Imagine a tricycle with the front wheel being your child and the two rear wheels being either parent. The front wheel steers but the back wheels provide balance. If the steering wheel is turned too far one way or the other, the trike will go in circles. When there is equilibrium, it can be pedaled nearly anywhere. As a child grows, he or she will graduate to a bicycle with training wheels. Usually, a child will lean on one side more than the other. Eventually, the training wheels are removed, and the child can manage independently. But the skill would be harder to master without the support of those two back training wheels.

Think of parenting as requiring the same kind of balance that exists in the tricycle, again with training wheels, and finally with a two-wheel bike. In the young stages of children's lives, they need the firmest support—a tricycle so to speak—in order to move forward because of the firm support of the back wheels. As a further analogy, remember you had to help your boy, for instance, steer his tricycle when he was first learning to ride.

As a child learns more about life, he or she graduates to training wheels. The two back wheels ideally represent more than one person in support of that child and should remain

there during the child's teenage years. Teenagers still need
support as they begin to balance on their own. Remember,
the training wheels are on both sides of the bike. Picture
them as providing a balance in child-rearing. A same-sex
parent offers a model for a child, yet an opposite-sex parent
is no less important. The latter will affect your children's
selection of a mate and provide a union that might one day
bring you the ultimate joy, a grandchild.

Finally, as young adults, your children are hopefully
ready to ride on their own. The training wheels are gone.
You no longer need to steer the bike. Your children can
pedal where they choose. And you can be sure they will
regularly pedal back to you. These are the children who
enjoy their parents after the nest is empty. These are also the
parents who carefully removed the training wheels.

There is no doubt that parenting is difficult. It is harder
if you are unhappy and/or you have to do it alone. Ordinarily after a divorce, the job is done alone although it does not
necessarily have to be so. Divorced couples can lose sight
of their child's needs when they alienate each other. You
cared enough about each other to share a bed at one point
in time. And as a result you created a child. Perhaps one of
you wanted a child without the other's consent. Maybe the
pregnancy was unplanned. None of that matters now. The
only concern is that you have a child, one who wants first
and foremost the love of both parents. How could that be
more than a child should expect?

There are plenty of unwanted children in this world. Too
many, really. Your child is valued by you. You would not be
reading this book if that were not so. You want to do what
is best, and if you have learned anything from what you have

read, it is that to do right by your child is one of the most difficult jobs you will face in life.

Take some measure of comfort in knowing that this is true for all parents, married or divorced. The issues discussed in this book are not solely in the realm of the divorced parent. Married parents are also often unhappy. They may compete with each other or put their needs first. They might not model what they want for their children, and they are sometimes cruel.

All any of us can do is make our best attempt to do a better job every day. We can strive to pay attention to our decisions. We can smile. We can choose happiness. We can decide to move our lives towards more love. And we can bring our children along for the ride.

....

CHALLENGE
Disrespect versus Mutual Regard

LESSON
Value those who value your child

CONCLUSION

Simple Wisdom for Parents

Fifty percent of the children living in the United States will experience the divorce of their parents before they are sixteen years old. This number has held constant for the past twenty years and is based on U.S. Census Bureau data. One and one-half million of our nation's children experience their parents' divorce every single year. This is an incredibly large number of children who experience a fracture to their families.

Another trend involves the sharp increase in the number of women purposely deciding to have a child without marrying. So we can't just look at the statistics of children living in single-parent homes as an indication of the number of children who have endured divorces. Some children may never know their father because their mothers have willfully created that situation. We also can't accurately analyze the data because fifteen percent of all children live in what we have come to call the blended family. These families defy any singular definition because the possible combinations, when considered, seem endless.

While writing this book, I have been unable to find anyone whose life has not been negatively touched by a divorce. Everyone has a story, and most of these stories are not pretty. It often seems as if the children are hurt the most. It is with passion and hope that I propose that this can stop.

Our children teach us about love by helping us understand our connection to them. But we have to be paying attention. And we have to perceive ourselves as closely as we are observing our children. Keeping your eye on your child is keeping your child's needs in focus. If you are shortsighted, you will not be as effective in teaching your child what he or she needs to know in order to thrive in the future. You will become cross-eyed if you lose sight of the boundaries that exist between parent and child. If you keep your eye on yourself, to the exclusion of your child, you may miss the signs your child is sending that might indicate he or she is struggling. You may be looking, but you will not see.

As a final closure to this book, I want to propose eight simple ideas that I believe sum up what I hope each reader will take away from this book. When we adhere to them, I believe all of us will make fewer mistakes with our children.

Number 1: Want what is best for the higher good

This involves doing what is best, not what is easiest. When we do what we know to be "right," it is almost always more difficult than many of our other options would be. This applies not only to parenting but also to our own personal growth as human beings. There is no question that effective parenting is easier when we work at improving ourselves. We can keep one eye on the children and the other on ourselves to help our children learn that becoming the best person possible is a lifelong challenge. A great beginning is to help our kids worry less by telling them that the love of both parents is a constant presence in their lives. All children will be comforted by this.

Number 2: Apologize to your children when you make a mistake

I have done plenty of apologizing to my children over the years. When I was too quick to make a judgment, if I said something that wasn't very nice, I said, "I am sorry." I also taught my children to strive to be the better person when they had disagreements with other people. I told them, "Don't stoop to someone else's level. You should apologize first when you need to."

I also apologized to my children for the fact that their father and I could not stay married. I told them I didn't plan to become a single mother, and that there were aspects of their lives that were not their fault. I also expected my daughters to deal with those less-than-ideal aspects as best they could. I did not allow them to use my divorce as an excuse for what they did not like in their lives. I expected them to cope, and they did.

Number 3: Check up on your children's stories

Children tell lies. It is one of the ways they test our resolve as parents. So follow up on what your child tells you, especially if there is any nagging uncertainty on your part. When you do this, you will catch your child deceiving you. When talking about this, always tell your child that your love for him or her does not go away because you are angry. Inherent in this is your personal level of honesty with your child. Tell your child about your feelings in terms he or she can understand, and do so with compassion for the difficulties that exist for all children.

Number 4: As often as you can, know where your children are and whom they are with

Once your child is a teenager and old enough to be home alone, you can't make the assumption that a responsible person has suddenly emerged unless you know that for yourself. The attitude that your children's actions aren't your problem when your child isn't with you implies that your love disappears when you are not together. Good parents understand that a child's freedom has to be tied to his or her level of responsibility. That is why most toddlers require extra vigilance. They don't understand the world but are often clever in acting out to get what they want. Older children quickly learn how to manipulate their parents to get what they want. And teenagers think they understand that which is impossible for them to know. They are no less clever than youngsters in the area of manipulation. They will tell each parent something different because they believe it will buy them more freedom.

Number 5: Have fun with your children

The life your child leads will impact the type of person he or she will become. Enjoy your children. It is as simple as that.

It is also helpful to meet your child's friends. Until your child can provide his or her own transportation, carpooling is a reality of life. You may be surprised that most teenagers in the backseat of your car will assume you can't drive and listen simultaneously. You'll be amazed at what you learn. And teenagers are funny. They enjoy laughing with their friends and usually are willing to include a parent who is open to their sense of humor. Just beware of the tendency to act "cool" in front of your teenager. Teens are usually embarrassed by this, and your discipline may be disregarded when you act like a peer because you may also be treated like one.

Number 6: Teach your child to avoid mistakes by looking at potential consequences before taking action

Decision-making is a skill. It can be learned. As a nurse, I learned to make decisions using the nursing process. It became so ingrained in my mind that I make all of my decisions using this process. It is automatic at this point. I taught my children to make decisions using many of these same principles.

The first step in decision-making "nursing style" is assessment. This involves looking at a situation from as many angles as possible. Second, make a plan. I told my children to "Minimize the potential downside. Don't close yourself off by your decisions." Step three is implementing your plan. If you have completed steps one and two, you have some idea of what will happen when you take action. Finally, evaluate the outcome. It sounds simple, but it isn't. Perhaps our most important job as parents is to teach our children to avoid mistakes. It may be true that this is our most important job as adults as well.

It is also possible to learn from the mistakes of others. You don't have to get arrested for drunk driving to learn that it is a mistake. You don't have to amass huge amounts of debt to realize that being responsible about your finances is a wise decision. And, you don't have to repeat your patterns in relationships unless you are content with how you share your love with others. You can and should learn about life from those around you, but you will first need to understand who *you* are.

Number 7: Celebrate time, not money

Money is often given too much power after a divorce. Money can buy nice things, but it can never buy happiness. When a divorced parent resents the possessions of others, envy results. Envy doesn't want what others have as much as it wants to take something away from someone else. This mirrors the possessiveness that some parents have when they don't want their children to gain new positive emotions toward a new stepmother or stepfather. This is another type of envy that tells a child that if they love their mother's new husband, for example, there is less love instead of more.

The irrationality of this thinking is rooted in the idea that there is only so much love to go around. Some people use this scarcity mentality whenever they compare their lives with others'. If your ex-spouse is happier now than when you were married, this takes nothing away from you because once you and your ex-spouse separated, your bond becomes your child, not your lives. An ex-husband or -wife's life impacts you only to the extent it affects your child. You have to intervene if your child is not being cared for. You should intervene if you are concerned about the values your child is learning from his or her other parent. You should not intervene if you suspect you are not *moving right*. You may be stuck in negative emotions that are moving you away from love.

If your neighbor has a nicer car than you that doesn't mean you can't also have a nice car. Someone else's wonderful job doesn't mean you can't also find a job you love. Your ex-spouse's happiness doesn't mean you can't also be happy. There is abundance in the world when we know it exists. When you look at the world and celebrate what you have, your world is beautiful. If you look at the world and focus on what is missing, you will lose even more. This is because we move toward what we think about. *Move right* and you will have more happiness. If you don't, you can guarantee more misery for yourself as well as your child.

We cannot teach our children about love and forgiveness if we don't live our lives according to the principles of goodness. This is related to the concept that what we see in others mirrors what we see in ourselves. If you tend to see the worst in others, you are also focusing on the worst within you. If you do this with your ex-spouse, you are investing too much of your personal energy on a relationship that will never be rewarding for you. Instead, focus on your child and the love you feel and strive to do this without comparing your love with the love from others. We love our children to the highest degree possible and when we can celebrate all the love in our children's lives we expand our own lives as well.

Number 8: Require your child to treat all adults with respect

Finally, treat everyone in your child's life with respect. And if you can't feel it, then act as if you do. This may seem to be in contrast with the authentic nature of expressing love, but it isn't. One of the most effective strategies of change is to begin to "act as if" you already possess that which you desire.

There is another component of this principle that is especially important for children. When you act as if you respect others, even when there is some small part of you that doesn't want to do that, you are showing your child that you are able to do difficult things even when you don't want to. One of the most important things we teach our children is that life includes having to do plenty of things we would rather not have to do.

Final Words

Most of us feel awful when we realize we have said or done something that has hurt our children. It shatters their foundation. And every child from every family in every country in the world has had instances in which they have felt frightened and insecure. It's an inherent part of childhood and cannot be entirely avoided. This is why there is no such thing as an ideal childhood.

Childhood can't be ideal because we, the parents, may try our very best at all times but we will still make mistakes. So will our children. There are no perfect parents, children, or families. Each family falls somewhere on the dysfunction scale. And it does not matter who lives where or is married to whom. What matters is how love is communicated to each and every member of the family.

When a divorce occurs in the life of a child, the child will wonder what happened to his or her parents' marriage. Even adults whose parents divorce will experience some hardship, and if these adults have children of their own, their children will become a part of the divorce of their grandparents. None of this means that the people involved love you or your child any less. But don't be surprised if it doesn't feel that way at times.

Trusting the person you could not stay married to is not easy. But your children's happiness will be influenced by your relationship with their other parent. As an example, can you honestly judge your ex-husband's love for your kids to be less valuable than your own simply because you divorced him? If so, you are moving away from love and you are

taking your children with you. Instead, work on remember-
ing that no one is going to love your children one iota less
now than before. Do *you* love them less? Of course not.

You cannot possibly love your kids for both yourself and
your ex-spouse. Likewise, your children won't love you twice
as much if you keep them away from a father or mother who
loves them too. Less love anywhere is less love everywhere.
The clingy child of divorce is frightened that love is going
away. But love can't go away without someone willfully
working toward that end. This should never happen in the
life of a child.

Once divorced, your goal is to gain the necessary
distance from an ex-spouse that will allow you to separate
emotionally while encouraging your child to maintain a
connection to both parents. In other words, you want to
strive to be happily divorced. You can start by accepting that
if there had been contentment in your marriage, the divorce
would not have happened.

When we understand our marriage for what it was,
we will realize we do not want this type of marriage for
ourselves. We want connections with others that are based
on consideration and respect, and few divorces encompass
these emotions. This has nothing to do with your child.
Treat your child's other parent with the same common
courtesy you would show a complete stranger, and you
are displaying simple human decency that will encourage
more love. I doubt any parent loves the half of their child
that comes from him or her and cares little for the half that
came from the other parent. I wonder how many children of
divorce understand that.

Our children's issues deserve our concern. We can all
work at expanding love, and it can start at home with our

children. Is it more difficult after divorce? Maybe. But also maybe not. Opening your child's life might also open your own because love and goodness can be found in the most surprising places. Most important, when you trip up—and you will—admit your mistake. Tell your child you are trying to be a better person every day. This will encourage your child to want to do the same. And be gentle with yourself. This will make it easier to be gentle with others.

Each of us is imperfect. So in essence, the first person you need to forgive is yourself. This is done when you do not let your mistakes define who you are. Instead, let success define you. This does not mean that you haven't made mistakes. You have, and you will continue to do so. The goal is to accept responsibility for your regrets and vow to make fewer mistakes in the future.

Therein lies the beauty of love—acceptance of who we are while working to be all we can be. We accomplish this when we accept our faults and work to overcome them. We also want to share our lives with those with similar beliefs about love and forgiveness. Perhaps that is what was missing in your marriage. There was not enough love or forgiveness between you and your ex-spouse to encourage acceptance. But the love for your child has not changed.

When we see our children's limitations, we are aware of our love for them. In fact, we are often most tuned in to our love when we watch our children struggle. We can strive for that same level of compassion for everyone we know. Celebrate that, and you will be celebrating more love. I make the prediction that when you accept others for who they are, including your ex-spouse, you will welcome more love for your child, and you are likelier to find more for yourself.

Common Questions

How do I start to change my behavior when I am dealing with my ex-spouse?

You have to decide if your desire for change outweighs the difficulty in making different decisions. If you decide that you can live with your current relationships as they are, things in your life will likely stay the same. If you decide that you want your life to be different, you will have to make a purposeful decision to change. This is when the difficult work begins.

Where should I begin?

Begin with your child.

I don't want to start acting differently. It will seem weird.

Then come to accept your life as it is today.

How do I begin?

You begin by learning to listen to your thoughts. This will help you understand whether your motives will encourage you to *move right*.

When is a good time to start?

When you are sick and tired of experiencing unhappiness.

Why is change so difficult?

Change involves the unknown and that is scary.

Is there an easy way?

Not if you want things to be different. Plenty of the messes people make in their lives are because they have convinced themselves that it is easier to leave things as they are. Deciding to not make your life better is still a decision. It is a decision to do nothing, and this often results in life getting even more difficult or unhappy.

I'm not sure I can do this.

All any of us can do is try. It may seem like common sense to admit that there have been times when we know we could have done better. I propose another way of looking at this. Perhaps we are all doing the best we can at any given moment. The best possible thing that comes out of any negative situation is that we learn to act differently in the future.

My divorce was so long ago. I acted in ways I now regret. What am I supposed to do now?

It is never too late to learn to be more open with others. You can begin by telling your child you are sorry about some of the things you said or did. Perhaps your child will share his or her reaction with you. In that case, the healing has already begun. If your child initially rejects your attempts, understand that you will have to go forward with determination. Be honest about your own feelings. But do this without attempting to make your child feel sorry for you. That can only happen when you are sure you are not feeling sorry for yourself.

But I do feel sorry for myself.

Begin by trying to forgive yourself for your shortcomings. Be compassionate when you consider that your life has been challenging and that all of us fall short at times. If you consider how deeply you love your child, begin to try and love yourself with that same intensity. You know your child is not perfect, but you love him or her anyway. Now consider that your child is also capable of loving an imperfect parent. After all, you know your own parents were not perfect and you love them anyway. In other words, love is the greatest compliment one imperfect person can give to another.

Why do we sometimes act mean?

All of us have good and bad within us. Everything we do or say moves us one way or the other. That is why it is so important to examine our inner selves. We can then make a conscious choice to move toward goodness.

How will I know what I am doing is working?

You will feel happier.

My ex-spouse is really irresponsible.

Go back to the point in time when you had the highest level of respect for this person. Ask yourself what happened in his or her life that led to this irresponsibility. More important, work to understand what, if any, role you played. Then perhaps you can begin to help your child's other parent to be more conscientious by involving them to the highest degree possible.

But if I do that my divorce doesn't make sense anymore.

Whenever we help another human being, our lives are enriched. We welcome more love into our lives when we help others experience more happiness.

This all seems like too much work.

Then get used to your life as it is now. If you are less happy than you used to be, then go back to a time of more happiness and work to recreate some of those aspects in your life.

A FEW EXAMPLES OF SOME OF THE QUESTIONS YOUR CHILD MAY ASK.

Why did you get divorced?

We couldn't be happy together anymore. Adult relationships are complicated. Sometimes things happen that seem like they can't be fixed.

Do you hate Mom [Dad]?

Of course not. I care about everyone in your life.

Then why couldn't you stay married?

I am sorry. I wish it could be different for you. Together we will try and make the best of it.

I don't want to go.

Let's talk about that. Tell me why.

I really don't like your new friend.

Please help me understand what you don't like.

Why did this happen to me?

It happened to us, all of us. And I will do my best to make it as easy as possible for you. Even so, it won't be easy. I hope all of us can be happier one day. But we are still a family because we care about each other. We have to remember that every single day.

Discussion questions

1. What has been your biggest challenge as a divorced parent?

2. When you look at the challenges presented on page seven of the book, where do you feel most vulnerable?

3. What have you handled relatively well since your divorce?

4. On a scale of one to ten, how do you think your child has coped with your divorce?

5. How about you?

6. Can you identify one area in which you would like to do a better job?

7. What would the first step be?

8. What will keep you from making that first step?

9. What would help you?

10. Find as least three examples of divorces you have witnessed where the child paid a higher price than necessary.

11. Find three more examples when the outcome was more positive for a child.

12. What did your divorce teach your child about love and forgiveness?

13. Did you relate personally to any of the stories in the book? If so, which ones and why.

INDEX

About the Author

Cheryl Grabenstein was an RN for 25 years, focusing on maternal child education and program development. She has conducted stress management seminars and started one of the first health education programs in the country. Cheryl received her Bachelor of Science degree in nursing from Old Dominion University in 1980 and holds a Masters of Education in Counseling from George Mason University. She is also a member of the elite Johns Hopkins Fellows Program.

Cheryl was recently a featured guest on the cable television program, Relatively Speaking. She lives with Larry, her husband of fifteen years, in Silver Spring, and Easton, Maryland.

Contact Information

Cheryl Grabenstein
4041 Powder Mill Road, Suite 205
Calverton, MD 20705

phone: 301-570-8020
email: info@thedivorcedparentschallenge.com
www.thedivorcedparentschallenge.com